Cayos y Baxos del Marques

40

26

18

46

10

37

36

30

28

36

40

Boca GRANDE

-2σG

White Sand

160

130

Flo

Ebb

Treasure
of the
Atocha

Treasure
of the
Atocha

by R. Duncan Mathewson III,
Archaeological Director of the
Search for the Nuestra Señora de Atocha

Foreword by Mel Fisher

With Photographs by Don Kincaid and Pat Clyne

Published in conjunction with Seafarers Heritage Library

 Pisces Books , New York

ILLUSTRATION CREDITS

Black and White Photos: 52 *top*, Don Kincaid; 52 *bottom*, Courtesy of Gene Lyon; 53, Don Kincaid; 56, Lawson Little; 60, Mitch Marken; 61, Pat Clyne; 74, Lawson Little; 75, Don Kincaid; 82—83, Lawson Little; 100—101, Lawson Little; 134, Pat Clyne; 135, Don Kincaid; 136—137, Pat Clyne.

Black and White Illustrations: 20—21, Bill Muir; 28—29, Unknown; 38—39, Bill Muir; 53, 56, Queen's Museum, Flushing, New York; 57, Jerry Cash; 60—61, D. Larissa Dillin; 74, Bill Muir; 100, D. Larissa Dillin; 106, 107 *bottom*, Syd Jones; 107, *top*, Bill Muir; 118—119, Ed Little; 136—137, D. Larissa Dillin.

Color Photos and Illustrations: C-1 *map*, Courtesy of Betty Bruce, Monroe County Library; C-2—C-4, *maps*, Dan Kouw; C-5—C-7, Don Kincaid; C-6 *ill.*, Jerry Cash; C-8 *top*, Don Kincaid; C-8 *bottom*, Pat Clyne; C-9, C-10 *top left & right*, Don Kincaid; C-10 *bottom*, Queen's Museum, Flushing, New York; C-11 *ill.*, D. Larissa Dillin; C-11 *bottom*, Pat Clyne; C-12—C-17, C-18 *bottom*, Don Kincaid; C-12, C-16 *ills.*, D. Larissa Dillin; C-18 *top*, C-19 *bottom*, Pat Clyne; C-19 *top*, Wendy Tucker; C-20—C-21, Don Kincaid; C-22, Pat Clyne; C-23, Prado Museum, Madrid, Spain; C-24, Pat Clyne; C-24 *ill.*, D. Larissa Dillin; C-25—C-26, Don Kincaid; C-27, Pat Clyne; C-27, *ill.*, D. Larissa Dillin; C-28—C-29, Don Kincaid; C-28—C-30 *ills.*, D. Larissa Dillin; C-30—C-32, Pat Clyne;. C-33—C-35, Don Kincaid; C-34 *ill.*, Henry Taylor III; C-35 *bottom right ill.*, Jerry Cash; C-36, Robert Holland; C-37—C-46, Don Kincaid; C-39, C-41, and p. C-44 *ills.*, Bill Muir; C-46—C-47 *ills.*, D. Larissa Dillin; C-47, C-48 *top left*, Pat Clyne; C-48 *top right*, Robert Holland; C-48 *bottom left & right*, C-49, Don Kincaid; C-50 *top*, Joe Bereswill; C-50 *bottom*, C-51, Don Kincaid; C-52 *top*, Robert Holland; C-52 *bottom*, C-53, Don Kincaid; C-54—C-55, Bill Raymond; C-56, Don Kincaid; C-57, C-58 *top*, Robert Holland; C-58 *bottom*, Pat Clyne; C-59 *top*, Don Kincaid; C-59 *bottom*, Craig Boyd; C-60 *top left & right*, Joe Bereswill; C-60 *bottom*, Robert Holland; C-61 *top left & right*, Pat Clyne; C-61 *bottom*, Robert Holland; C-62 *top*, Don Kincaid; C-62 *bottom*, C-63, Pat Clyne; C-64 *top*, Don Kincaid; C-64 *bottom*, Robert Holland.

This book was published in conjunction with Seafarers Heritage Library Ltd.

Library of Congress Cataloging-in-Publication Data

Mathewson, R. Duncan
   Treasure of the Atocha

   Includes index
   1. Nuestra Senora de Atocha (ship) 2; Treasure-trove--Florida. 1. Title
G530.N83M38   1986   975.9   85-30978
ISBN 0-86636-044-1

Printing and Binding by
Toppan Printing Co. (H.K.) Ltd.

Typesetting by Vera-Reyes, Inc.

Printed in Hong Kong

10 9 8 7 6 5 4 3 2 1

This book is dedicated to members of my family—both past and present generations—particularly my father, who passed on to me his own father's love of the sea, and my mother who first encouraged me to become an archaeologist.

Acknowledgement

"It is of great importance that the general public be given the
opportunity to experience, consciously and intelligently, the
efforts and the results of scientific research. It is not sufficient
that each result be taken up, elaborated, and applied by a few
specialists in the field. Restricting the body of knowledge to a
small group deadens the philosophical spirit of a people and leads
to spiritual poverty."

Albert Einstein

It's impossible to adequately acknowledge all the people who
made this book possible. I first need to express my gratitude and appreciation to Mel and Dolores Fisher and to the others at Treasure Salvors, Inc.
who helped pull the research together. Special thanks go to the boat captains, divers, and crew members—they are too numerous to mention here
individually, but their patience, knowledge, and cooperation greatly facili-
tated the recovery of archaeological data on the site over the past 12 years.
Through their active participation they've made invaluable contributions
toward achieving a better archaeological understanding of the 1622 sites
than would otherwise have been impossible.

Above all else, I am greatly indebted to Dr. Eugene Lyon for
unhesitatingly sharing with me the fruits of his archival research on the
1622 *Flota* and for allowing me to quote from his published and unpub-
lished works. His 1979 book, *The Search for the Atocha,* provided an invaluable base for the narrative of the historical research on these ships. My
collaboration with Gene since 1973 has been an enjoyable and stimulat-
ing learning experience for which I am deeply grateful.

Major contributions to archaeological research on this site have been made by a number of scholars from the academic community and from museum specialists who have assisted in the recovery and interpretation of data. Members of the research team are listed in the appendix along with the people of Treasure Salvors who are continuing to make major contributions.

Special acknowledgement is due Herb and Cora Taylor of Pisces Books and my partner, William J. Ryan, of Seafarers Heritage Library, for their help in bringing this work to the public. I also wish to express my deep appreciation to Steve Blount and Lisa Walker of Communications Design for their skillful editorial efforts in shaping and preparing the manuscript, and to Carol Denby and everybody on the production staff of Pisces Books. Sincere thanks go to Chloe Schroder, and Jeanne Bauer who, over the years, very patiently prepared many of my notes and research material.

Appreciation is also due those friends, colleagues, and family members who helped me shape the final version of the manuscript.

Perhaps the greatest treasure I have received over the years while studying the 1622 shipwrecks has been the friendships I have made with so many different types of people all over the country. The commonality of interests and ideas I've shared with salvors, archaeologists, sport divers, academics, and public officials have clearly shown that shipwreck archaeology has as much to do with understanding people as it does with understanding inanimate objects. These friendships have given me a tremendous lift; they are a great treasure trove of remembrances I will never be able to repay.

R. Duncan Mathewson III

Contents

Preface   *10*
   by R. Duncan Mathewson III

Foreword   *12*
   by Mel Fisher, President, Treasure Salvors, Inc.

Introduction   *14*

PART I

1. The Ghost Galleons   *18*
Spanish ships and treasure of the 1622 fleet. An account of their loss off the Florida Keys.

2. Archives and Artifacts   *25*
Historical records and important early finds provide essential clues about where the treasure lies.

3. The Search Begins   *31*
The underwater mystery deepens. Where is the Atocha?

PART II

4. Archaeological Challenge   *44*
Systematic underwater mapping and artifact research becomes a necessity. A new phase in the search begins.

5. Identifying the Wreck   *54*
Tantalizing discoveries positively identify the site but the main part of the wreck goes unfound.

6. The Deep Water Theory   *64*
A new idea is tested. The search widens.

7. History in Bronze   *70*
The cannons of the Atocha *are found. The main part of the wreck must be near.*

8. Exploring Hawk Channel   *80*
Search and survey operations produce new clues.

9. A Priceless Treasure   *88*
The Santa Margarita *is found. A big piece of the puzzle fits into place.*

10. The Motherlode   *97*
A reef of silver is discovered. Mel's 16 year quest is justified.

11. Archaeology on Trial   *116*
Struggles with government bureaucrats and academic archaeologists cloud the horizon.

PART III

Beyond the Glitter...Secrets Revealed   *126*
The maritime world of the Atocha *springs to life as artifacts speak of the glory and splendor of Spanish America during the early 17th Century.*

Epilogue   *143*

Appendices

1. *Treasure Salvors Inc.*   *146*
2. *Selected Bibliography*   *154*

Index   *158*

Preface

My introduction to historic shipwreck archaeology came one day in 1973 with a telegram from Mel Fisher, president of Treasure Salvors, Inc. For four years, Mel and his staff had been on the track of two Spanish galleons, heavily laden with gold and silver, known to have sunk in a hurricane somewhere in the Florida Keys in 1622. Now they needed an archaeologist to help piece together the physical evidence they were retrieving from the sea bed 20 miles west of Key West. Having worked in Africa and Jamaica for many years as a land archaeologist on English and Spanish colonial sites, I wasn't sure what to expect when I first met Fisher and his salvage crew.

As I learned more about the enormity of their task, I began to see many ways in which archaeological research and systematic mapping could help solve their problems. Dr. Eugene Lyon, a historian, had been researching the history of the two ships they were searching for, *Nuestra Señora de Atocha* and *Santa Margarita*, in the Spanish archives in Seville, Spain. This archival study successfully located the general area of the wrecks. Now, precise mapping on the sea bed was necessary to pinpoint their location. I soon became fascinated with the idea of turning this treasure hunt into an archaeological salvage operation by recording the archaeology of these shipwrecks in close collaboration with Lyon, who had already compiled a vast amount of documentation on the vessels.

I still recall my first dive on the *Atocha* site vividly. It was like being transported back in time, over 350 years, to the day this historic ship went down. Artifacts were spread over the site. In the sparkling blue waters of the Marquesas Keys, silver coins, bits of pottery, and swords were clearly visible to the trained eye. After I had swum across the site several times, I became aware of the rich archaeological information which seemed to surround me, scattered on the bottom. I had spent years digging in dirt, at times ecstatic by the find of a single metal object. This ship had carried nearly a quarter of a million coins. And no one knew what other artifacts—navigational instruments, weapons, religious objects—might be here that perhaps have never been uncovered anywhere else in the world. A rush of archaeological questions, for which I was quite unprepared, hammered my brain. The revelation of the richness of the cultural material on the *Atocha* site inspired a great wonderment for shipwreck archaeology from which I will never recover. It changed my life, and profoundly changed the course of my professional career.

Diving on the *Atocha* and *Margarita* has been an exhilarating learning experience. The slow but steady accumulation of information about these two galleons and their trove of archaeological treasures is enormous fun—a tortuously unraveling historical mystery. The years of research on these sites have opened my eyes to many questions about the archaeology of shipwrecks in American waters. Now I am happy to be able to share some of this accumulated knowledge with the public. I hope this book helps divers and non-divers alike to share some of the excitement I was privileged to experience on the *Atocha* site while trying to piece together one of the greatest archaeological jigsaw puzzles in the New World.

R. Duncan Mathewson III
Little Torch Key, Florida
November 1985

Foreword

All over the world, day after day, the sea is giving up her secrets. Shipwrecks are being discovered and artifacts are being recovered from these unique time capsules of history. For 16 long years I pursued a dream of finding the lost resting place of *Nuestra Señora de Atocha*. Many people didn't believe the dream, but those who stayed with me finally achieved what sceptics thought impossible.

Finding the "motherlode" of the *Atocha* never would have been possible without the many people who played essential roles in the search. Piecing together the archaeological jigsaw puzzle over ten miles of sea bed was not easy. It took everybody working together—Fay Feild, Don Kincaid, Bleth McHaley, Pat Clyne, Ed Little, Jim Sinclair, Jerry Cash, Bill Muir, D. Larissa Dillin, Leah Miguel, and my four children, Kim, Kane, Terry and Taffi, as well as other members of my family, boat captains and crew, and our laboratory and office staff—to make our dreams a reality. Crucial to this effort was the historical research carried out for many years by Dr. Eugene Lyon and the archaeological documentation compiled by R. Duncan Mathewson III. Working in close collaboration, these two scholars brought cultural meaning to the wonderful things my salvage divers were bringing up from the Marquesas.

When Duncan first joined our team in 1973, I really didn't know what to expect: I knew we needed a professional archaeologist, but my past experience with State archaeologists had left a bitter taste in my mouth about archaeology. Though Duncan and I did not always agree about how things should be done on the site, we became convinced that neither of us could do our job properly without cooperation from the other.

Solving the archaeological mysteries of the *Atocha* and her sister ship, the *Santa Margarita*, has been a great adventure for us all. This book provides an inside look at how the archaeological jigsaw puzzle slowly came together over many years. It is an exciting story in which all of us at Treasure Salvors, Inc., are proud to have played a part. I hope it inspires adventurous people all over the country who dare to dream the impossible. Let's all work together to ensure that we will always have the opportunity to search for our own treasures—wherever they may be. There is still much to learn about shipwrecks in the Americas; but one thing is for certain, the best wrecks have yet to be found. Good diving to you all!

Mel Fisher, *President*
Treasure Salvors, Inc.

Today's the day!

Introduction

Marquesas Keys, Florida, July 20, 1985: "Put away the charts! We found it!" Kane Fisher's voice crackled out of the radio at the Key West office of Treasure Salvors, the salvage company owned by his father, Mel Fisher. The announcement set off an instant, nearly riotous, celebration.

Kane Fisher spoke from the deck of the *Dauntless*, a salvage boat which had been combing the ocean floor off Key West for the wreckage of a Spanish galleon, *Nuestra Señora de Atocha*. Today's the day that Treasure Salvors' 16-year search finally yields the solution to a 350-year-old mystery. The silver ingots—over 1,000 of them stacked like a cord of wood—mark the resting place of the bulk of the cargo of the *Atocha*, which sank during a hurricane in 1622.

During that 16 years, Mel Fisher often encouraged his divers by telling them, "Today's the day." He even had the phrase printed on t-shirts. And that hope kept them going through times when there was no money to pay their wages, through the weary months between the tantalizing finds of a single silver ingot or a scrap of jewelry.

Ironically, today is also the day, July 20, marking the tenth anniversary of the death of Mel's oldest son, Dirk, Dirk's wife, Angel, and crewman Rick Gage. The three drowned when the company's salvage tug *Northwind* capsized. Three days before his death, Dirk had located a pile of bronze cannons. Those cannons confirmed that the scattered artifacts the divers had been finding for the past four years were part of the long-lost *Atocha*.

Now, a decade later, the fervent optimism of Mel Fisher, and the skill of a dedicated band of archaeologists, scientists, historians, sailors, and divers had finally uncovered the scene of one of Spain's most financially disastrous maritime accidents.

The hurricane that wrecked the *Atocha* was no more fierce than the forces spawned by Fisher's monomanical search.

In addition to the loss of lives, the search consumed $8 million dollars—profits from Fisher's earlier salvage of a fleet of galleons sunk in 1715 plus the funds of hundreds of investors.

In the treasure business, success can be more difficult than failure. During the 16-year search Fisher had to wage battle in court with the United States Federal Government and the State of Florida for ownership of the *Atocha's* great wealth.

In ruling against the United States and for Treasure Salvors in March 1978, Judge Walter P. Gewin of the U.S. Court of Appeals wrote: "This action evokes all the romance and danger of the buccaneering days in the West Indies. It is rooted in an ancient tragedy of Imperial Spain, and embraces a modern tragedy as well. The case also represents the story of triumph, a story in which the daring and determination of the colonial settlers are mirrored by contemporary treasure seekers."

Judge Gewins' ruling hints at the adventure of treasure hunting. Treasure is an almost universal human dream. While the stories of pirates that inspire the wistful longing for the bright gleam of gold chains, the dull lustre of fine silver, and the brilliance of a well-crafted emerald may be fiction, they have a firm foundation in fact.

For most of us, those stories remain dreams. But not for Mel Fisher, and not for the people who are Treasure Salvors, Inc. They fought the sea, the government, even modern-day pirates, to recover the wealth of the *Atocha*. In their search, they adapted every useful instrument of modern technology, following through with sweat in a dogged physical struggle with the capricious ocean. In the salvage of the *Atocha*, for the first time, the work of commercial salvors was guided by a team of historians and archaeologists. Despite the disparagement of other professional archaeologists who claimed the archaeological work done on the *Atocha* was useless because it was carried out by a commercial salvage company, the innovations and knowledge gained in the operation proved conclusively that shallow water shipwrecks in the New World could be uncovered with the same meticulous attention to detail exercised on sites on dry land. With details patiently pieced together from the rotted timbers and crushed jewelry and information gained from worm-eaten documents, the divers, historians, and archaeologists were able to add enormously to what is known about Spain's New World Colonies in the 17th century.

What follows is the story of an extraordinary group of men and women who followed their dream of locating underwater riches and succeeded where the power of Imperial Spain, Dutch warships, and English pirates failed.

PART
I

The Spanish Caribbean

An early 19th century English chart of the area west of the Marquesas Keys shows where the Atocha and Margarita sank. The early 17th century Spanish name, "Cayos y Baxos del Marques" denotes the Quicksands area.

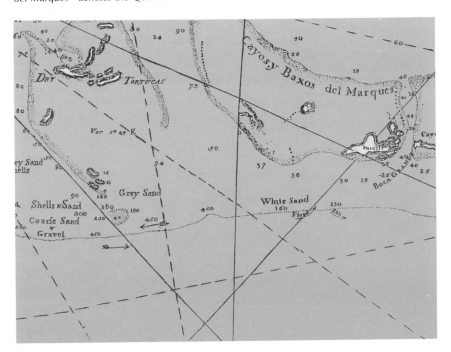

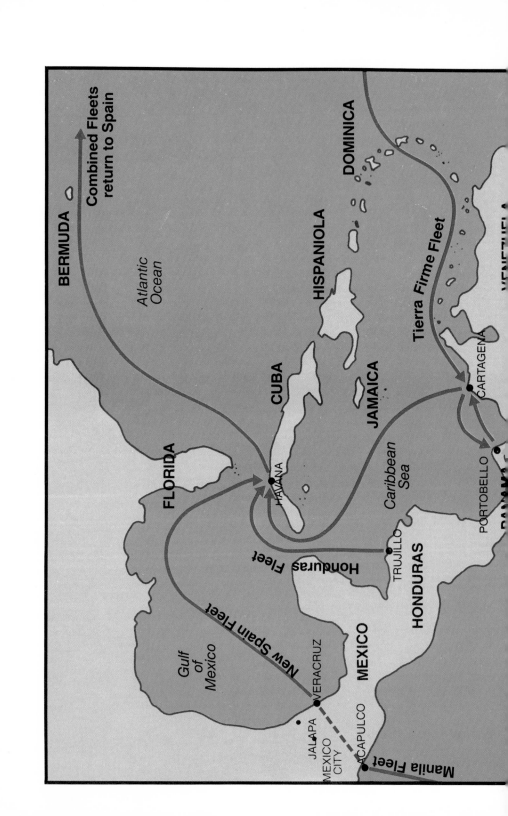

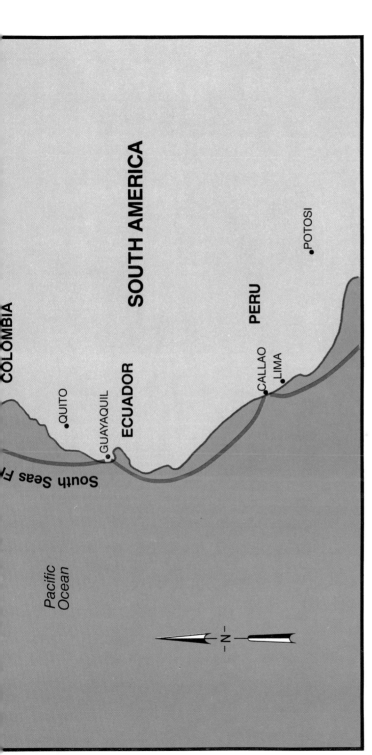

SOUTH AMERICA

COLOMBIA

ECUADOR

•QUITO

•GUAYAQUIL

PERU

CALLAO•
•LIMA

•POTOSI

Pacific
Ocean

South Seas Fl

N

In the early spring of 1622, a convoy sailed from Spain, and upon arriving
in the Caribbean dispersed into groups to pick up heavy consignments of
royal and private treasure.
   Each fleet, or flota, had a specific destination. The Tierra Firme fleet,
which the Atocha and Margarita were a part of, was loaded in Portobello
and Cartagena with silver and gold from Peru, Ecuador, and Colombia;
emeralds from Colombia; pearls from Venezuela. The Honduras fleet
called at Trujillo for valuable indigo dye, and other agricultural products.

The Manila fleet sailed from the Philippines to deliver fine china, porcelain,
silk, and other products of Spain's trade in the Orient to Acapulco. The
cargo was then transported overland to Veracruz, on the east coast of Mexico.
At Veracruz, it was picked up by the New Spain fleet along with gold and
silver from the Royal mint at Mexico City.
   The fleets would then meet in Havana, Cuba to assemble the cargo for
the voyage back to Spain.

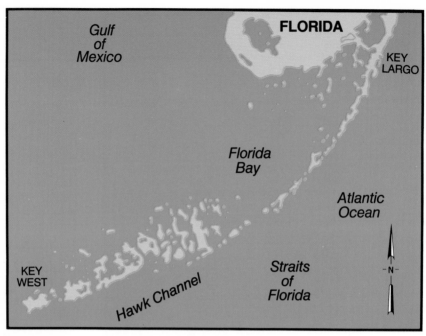

The Florida Keys from Key Largo to Key West. The islands were originally called Matecumbe by the Spanish.

The tip of the Florida Keys from Key West to the Dry Tortugas. This was the area where the 1622 fleet was wrecked.

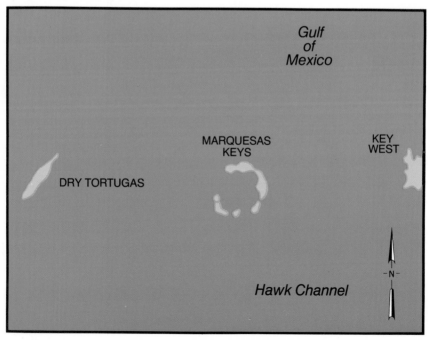

"The Admiral of the whole fleet (Atocha) following the storm,
and driven by the wind with the fore-sail of the middle most mast,
ran Northward all night and the next day, whereupon they proposed
to rest in some harbor, or place of security on those shores: but
suddenly they came to shallow water, and in short space ran herself
on ground (in) two fathom water and a little more, where her beak
broke into pieces, with the loss of her people, except three men and
two boys: This was on the coast of Maracambe (Matecumbe) in
Florida. The Galeon Margarita followed the same course and
participated with the same fortune."

English account translated from
Spanish document, 1623

ᗡꑇ chapter 1 ᗒ᠎ᗞ

The Ghost Galleons

In the century following Columbus' dramatic voyage of discovery in 1492, the riches of her New World colonies helped make Spain the most powerful nation in Europe. Taxes on goods shipped from Central and South America by Spanish merchants enabled Spain to defend its Western Hemisphere claims against the English, French, and Dutch, and to extend its empire halfway around the world into the South Pacific.

The *Atocha* and its sister ship, *Santa Margarita*, are tragic milestones along this broad commercial highway (called *Carrera de Indias* by the Spanish) that carried Europe on a journey from isolation to world domination. Not only were the colonies prime consumers of goods produced in Spain; the conquests initiated a torrent of valuable agricultural goods, precious metals and high-quality gems that pulsed through the veins of Spanish mercantile shipping and back to the mother country. From 1530 to 1800, approximately six billion to eight billion dollars of gold and silver were mined in the Spanish American colonies. During this time, the ratio of gold to silver shipped to Spain was about one to ten. This wealth drastically changed the course of European history, raising Spain to a position of world dominance.

When 16-year-old Philip IV ascended the throne in 1621, he inherited an empire that controlled vast territories on four continents, a mission to purge Europe of the growing threat of Protestantism, and a huge national debt.

The trade with the Indies, and the taxes and revenues the Crown derived from it, were the financial lifeline which kept the Empire—and its staunch defense of Catholicism—afloat. The threats to this lifeline were legion. The Dutch openly attacked the Indies fleets. The English and French continuously challenged Spain's claims in the New World. And internally, Spanish merchants engaged in smuggling, bribery, and deceit to avoid paying the *quinto*, a 20% tax levied on the proceeds of trade with the Indies.

In 1503, a regulatory agency was established to oversee every aspect of Spain's trade with the Indies. Called the *Casa de Contrastacion*, it functioned both as ministry of commerce and official school of navigation. A clerk, or *escribano*, accompanied each vessel and maintained the official record of all cargo loaded and unloaded: the ship's manifest. The manifest served as the basis for collecting the *quinto* and the *averia*, an additional tax, as high as 40% helped the government offset the cost of defending the merchant vessels that brought Indies wealth to Spain.

To discourage smuggling, the Crown decreed in 1510 that smugglers would forfeit their contraband and pay a fine of four times its value. Naval officers convicted of smuggling could be sentenced to several years as a galley slave. Despite the tough laws, it's estimated that more than 20 percent of the gold and silver mined in the New World was smuggled back to Spain untaxed.

To minimize losses to armed raiders, Spain required all merchant ships to sail in convoys, which were protected by escort ships known as galleons. The galleons were a special type of warship, up to a hundred feet long and rigged with square sails. The profile was unmistakable, as the stern section of a galleon, called the sterncastle, soared up to 35 feet above the ship's waterline, and was capped with the classic high poop deck. And the galleons were heavily armed, mounting huge bronze cannons. Although slower than the quick brigantines and sloops favored by pirates, the galleons possessed immense firepower. Still, perhaps five percent of the silver and gold mined by Spain in the New World was lost at sea or confiscated by pirates. In addition to the galleons sailing among the merchant ships in convoy, two strong galleons—a *capitana*, which led the group, and an *almiranta*, which brought up the rear—provided extra protection against English, French, and Dutch raiders. The convoys sailed from Spain in early spring and, upon arriving in the Caribbean, dispersed into groups to pick up heavy consignments of Royal treasure from various ports in the colonies.

Each fleet, or *flota*, had a specific destination. The Manila fleet sailed from the Philippines and delivered fine china, porcelain, silk, and other products of Spain's trade in the Orient to Acapulco. The cargo was then transported overland to Veracruz, on the east coast of Mexico. At Veracruz, it was picked up by the New Spain fleet along with gold and silver from the Royal mint at Mexico City.

The *Tierra Firme* fleet was loaded in Portobello and Cartagena with silver and gold from Peru, Ecuador, Venezuela, and Colombia. Copper from the King's mines in Cuba was added in Havana. The

Bill Muir, a shipwreck historian and draftsman, used photos, measurements, and the original contract specifications to draft a preliminary reconstruction of the Atocha. Built in Havana, Cuba in 1620 by Alonso Ferreira, Master Shipwright, the Spanish Guard galleon weighed 550 tons. The lines of the ships—the raised forecastle, towering sterncastle, square sails, and long bowsprit—mark her as a typical galleon. The lower hull ends just below the line of gunports, and everything above it is superstructure. This modular construction made galleons susceptible to breaking into numerous parts during or after they sank.

Honduras fleet called at Trujillo for valuable indigo dye.

When things went according to plan, all fleets met in Havana, Cuba in July to assemble the cargo for the voyage back to Spain. The bulk of the gold and silver was usually carried by the large, heavily-armed galleons, while the smaller merchant ships transported agricultural products.

Spain was still the preeminent power in 1622. However, her position of power was badly slipping as the crucial stages of the Thirty Years War unfolded. The year before, Spain had ended a 12-year truce with her rebellious Dutch provinces. The Dutch had joined with France, openly attacking Spanish naval and merchant vessels. The cost of the fighting sapped Spain's economy, and the Royal Treasury was seriously overextended. To finance the war and continue the pomp and splendor of the Royal Court, the Crown borrowed heavily; so heavily that the king's bankers kept representatives in Seville to claim a large share of the wealth when the rich convoys arrived from the New World each year.

Although the treasure fleet had sailed in 1621, money in the treasury was dangerously low. Collected taxes and royal proceeds accumulating in the Americas were desperately needed. It was paramount that the 1622 fleet successfully make the long and dangerous voyage. The government's creditors were impatient, and the king's share of the treasure would keep them at bay a bit longer. It might even convince them to extend more badly needed funds for the war effort.

Despite the urgent need, the fleet could only begin its voyage in late spring or early summer. The Atlantic is hospitable to sailing ships only a few months each year. Winter storms in the North Atlantic made the trip to the Americas dangerous if taken before early spring. And from June to October, the South Atlantic routes traveled by the convoys on their journey back to Spain from Havana were racked by hurricanes. Lashed by mammoth seas, ships ambushed by a hurricane could neither steer nor sail. They could merely run in front of the wind and hope it blew itself out before the ship was swamped or her hull was torn open on a shallow coral reef. The later in the summer the fleets sailed from Havana, the more likely they were to encounter a major hurricane. If the convoys waited out the hurricane season in the harbor at Havana— leaving in late October or November—they risked sailing into the violent winter storms of the North Atlantic.

This year, the flotas left Spain separately: the *Tierra Firme* fleet, including the heavily-armed *Nuestra Señora de Atocha*, left March 23, 1622, arriving at Portobello on the Isthmus of Panama on May 24. Seven Guard galleons, including the *Santa Margarita*, sailed from Cadiz on April 23, arriving at the island of Dominica on May 31. There, 16 smaller vessels fanned out to pick up goods from around the Caribbean while the Guard galleons sailed to Cartagena, Colombia to unload their outbound cargos, arriving on June 24. Finding that much of the silver and gold to be shipped back to Spain had not yet arrived at the port for loading, the Guard galleons sailed for Portobello, joining the *Tierra Firme* fleet there on July 1.

The commander of the Guard fleet, the Marquis of Cadereita, was told that 36 Dutch warships were at the Araya salt-pans on the north coast of South America. For extra protection he commandeered a privately owned galleon, *Nuestra Señora del Rosario*, to his Guard fleet, bringing it up to its full authorized strength of eight ships.

The ships left Portobello, arriving back in Cartagena on July 27. After receiving more cargo, they sailed for Cuba on August 3. Poor sailing conditions delayed their arrival, and the fleet didn't reach Havana until August 22. The presence of so many Dutch raiders must have weighed heavily on the Marquis' mind. The New Spain fleet had collected its cargo in Mexico and waited in Havana for the rest of the fleets. Now, as the most dangerous part of the hurricane season neared, its commander impatiently requested permission to sail for Spain. The Marquis assented, but directed that the bulk of the bullion and coins carried by the New Spain ships be held in Havana, to be shipped back under the protection of the big cannons of the Guard fleet.

The Marquis split his fleet into two parts. He would sail in the *capitana*, the lead ship, the *Nuestra Señora de Candeleria*. Much of the one and a half million pesos worth of treasure—a hoard worth today perhaps $400 million—was assigned to the *Santa Margarita* and a new ship, the *Nuestra Señora de Atocha*. The *Atocha* had been built in the Havana shipyard and, sure to bring her good luck, was named for the most revered religious shrine in Spain. Just in case the Almighty's providence didn't extend to sinking Dutch warships, the *Atocha* was fitted with 20 bronze cannons. This strong ship was to be the *almiranta*, sailing last to protect the slow, lumbering merchant ships in the rear of the *flota*. The *Tierra Firme* and Guard ships—28 vessels in all—departed from Havana on September 4, six weeks behind schedule.

Neither God's providence nor gunpowder could protect the ships from the weather.

On September 5, the fleets were overtaken by a rapidly-moving hurricane. As dawn streaked the horizon, it brought dread to the more experienced sailors. The gale force winds, rising out of the northeast, quickly increased. The gusts raked the surface of the northward-flowing Gulf Stream, piling up huge seas in front of the ships. Aboard the *Atocha*, the chief pilot lit a lantern as clouds and rain blackened the sky. Ahead, the lead galleons were already out of sight. The merchant ships sailing close by the *almiranta* were themselves hidden by rain as the storm swept by. Crewmen scrambled into the rigging to take in sail. As they hung from this fragile rope spider's web high above the deck, the ends of the yard arms dipped into the ocean as the ship rolled violently. Frothing green water roared across the deck. Just before darkness, a veil of spray closed around the seasick passengers and crew of the *Atocha*. They watched in horror as the tiny *Nuestra Señora de la Consolacion*, wallowing in the mammoth seas, simply capsized and disappeared.

That night, the wind shifted, coming out of the south. The hurricane now hurled the fleet north toward the Florida reef line. Before daylight, the Marquis' ship—the *Candeleria*—and 20 other vessels passed to the west of a group of rocky islands, the Dry Tortugas. Beyond the reefs of the Straits of Florida, they rode out the winds in the safe, deep waters of the Gulf of Mexico. Behind them, they'd left several small merchant vessels on the bottom in deep water. At least four ships, including the *Atocha* and *Santa Margarita*, were swept headlong into the Florida Keys. Near a low-lying atoll fringed with mangroves, 15-foot rollers carried the *Margarita* across the reef, grounding her in the shallows beyond. As she crossed the reef, her commander, Captain Bernardino de Lugo, looked to the east. There he saw the *Atocha*.

With crew and passengers huddled, praying below deck, the *Atocha* approached the line of reefs dividing safe, deep water from certain death. The frenzied crew dropped anchors into the reef face, hoping to hold the groaning, creaking galleon off the jagged coral. A wave lifted the ship, and, in the next instant, flung it down directly onto the reef. The main mast snapped as the huge seas washed *Atocha* off the reef and beyond, trailing her broken mast. Water poured through a gaping hole in the bow, quickly filling the hull with water. The great ship slipped beneath the surface, finding bottom 55 feet below; only the stump of the mizzenmast broke the waves. Of the 265 persons aboard, 260 drowned. Three crewmen and two black slaves clung to the mast until they were rescued the next morning by a launch from another fleet ship, the *Santa Cruz*.

The lost ships of the 1622 treasure fleet lay scattered over 50 miles stretching from the Dry Tortugas eastward to where the *Atocha* slipped beneath the water. About 550 people perished along with a total cargo worth more than 2 million pesos.

✑ *chapter 2* ✑

𝕬rchives and 𝕬rtifacts

On September 12, 1622, the Marquis of Cade-reita held a meeting attended by shaken survivors of the storm. Twenty of the 28 ships had returned to Havana. It was decided that the treasure fleet would stay in Havana while an attempt was made to salvage the *Atocha* and the *Margarita* which had carried the bulk of the fleet's treasure. Gaspar de Vargas, a veteran seaman, was dispatched later with five ships, salvage tackle, and divers. On September 17, Bartolome Lopez, owner of the frigate *Santa Catalina*, arrived in Havana after spotting the wreck of the *Atocha* near the last Key of Matecumbe. The Marquis sent Lopez to guide Vargas to the wrecks.

Lopez caught up with Vargas and they found the *Atocha* quickly, her mizzenmast still protruding above the water. The *almiranta* was down 55 feet—very deep for the salvage divers who could work only as long as the air in their lungs held out. The divers reported that the hatches and gunports were securely fastened. Unable to force their way into the hold, the divers could do no more than salvage two small iron swivel cannons off the deck. Vargas turned west, looking for the spot where the *Margarita* had gone aground and broken up. Failing to find the wrecksite, Vargas sailed further west to look for his ship, the *Rosario*. At Loggerhead Key, he found the hull of the *Rosario* and a small group of survivors who had waded ashore. They had spent three weeks marooned on the windswept islet, with little food or water.

Vargas burned the *Rosario* to the waterline, exposing her cargo—bullion, copper, and cannons—for quick salvage. After some initial success, on October 5 a second hurricane swept through the Florida Straits. Vargas and the survivors of the *Rosario*, facing their

second storm in as many months, moved to the highest ground on the
Key. The ocean surged up after them, but eventually receded. Quickly
finishing the work on the *Rosario*, Vargas returned to Havana for more
tools to salvage the *Atocha*.

Equipped with more divers, including pearl divers from the
island of Margarita, Vargas' crew camped on a small mangrove atoll
near the place where they had seen the wreck of the *Atocha*. But the
almiranta could not be found—her mizzenmast had disappeared. The
salvage crews dragged the bottom with grapnel hooks, hoping to snag a
part of the wreck. The crews rowed out to the wrecksite from the small
island again and again, sometimes three hours out and up to eight hours
back. The men's calloused palms, dried by the salt spray and rubbed
raw by the rough oar handles, split open as they struggled to push their
small boats through heavy swells kicked up by the blustery January
winds. Worse still, the bottom here was a bed of shifting sands which
moved at the slightest provocation. No doubt Vargas suspected that the
sands, stirred by the October hurricane and the winter storms, had
already covered the *Atocha*.

In February, the Marquis sailed from Havana to take charge
of the salvage efforts, setting up camp with Vargas on the small island.
The salvors renamed the atoll in his honor, calling it *Cayo de Marques*,
and redoubled their efforts. Although a few silver ingots were found, the
hull of the *Atocha* eluded them. In April, the Marquis returned to
Havana. There he found Captain Nicholas de Cardona and a team of
skilled divers who had arrived from Mexico to help with the salvage.
While the Marquis sailed for Spain with the long-delayed fleet, Cardona
sailed for the Keys, joining Vargas for the final salvage effort.

Each time the grapnel hooks caught on something, the divers
went over the side. Holding rocks to speed them down, they plunged
headfirst, eardrums snapping and popping from the increase in water
pressure as they descended. The deep water gave them precious little
time on the bottom, and even the experienced pearl divers were forced
to surface gasping for air time after time, their hands as empty as their
lungs. By August, Vargas was thoroughly discouraged. Leaving buoys
to mark the search area, the salvors returned to Havana and Vargas
for Spain. Nicholas de Cardona prepared a map of the search area for
the salvage report before he too left Havana.

The loss of the 1622 fleet was a disaster for the Royal Treasury.
The Crown was forced to borrow vast new sums from its already nervous
bankers to continue the Thirty Years War. Armed ships from Spain's
rebellious Dutch provinces pressed their attacks on Spanish maritime
trade. Despite these attacks, the merchants in charge of administering
the *averia* tax for the protection of the treasure convoys sold several
Guard galleons, raising cash to help cover the loss of the 1622 fleet. It
was imperative that the treasure of the *Margarita* and the *Atocha* be

found to bolster the faltering Royal Treasury and the merchants whose private purses had been crippled by the sinkings. But Gaspar de Vargas, as experienced a seaman as Spain had in the Indies, had given up hope of finding the galleons. Nicholas de Cardona, with his team of skilled divers, had given up. What was needed was an ambitious man with an equally ambitious plan for locating and salvaging the wrecks.

Nunez Melián was such a man. In 1624, the politician and adventurer was granted a contract to salvage the *Atocha* and the *Margarita*. It took Melián nearly two years to prepare for his effort. At a cost of 5,000 *reales*, he had a 680-pound copper diving bell cast to aid in the search. Once on site, in June 1626, the bell soon paid for itself. Juan Bañon, a slave, spotted wreckage through the diving bell's windows. Surfacing for a rope, he quickly returned to the bottom and brought up a silver ingot. The *Santa Margarita* was found!

News of the find spread quickly. No doubt it was greeted with enthusiasm at the Royal Court in Spain. It also sparked action among Spain's enemies. The Dutch and English were as interested in keeping the treasure out of Spain's coffers as in adding it to their own war chests. Piet Heyn, a Dutch admiral, soon arrived in the Caribbean with 30 warships. Raiding parties interrupted Melian's work three times over the next four years but, in between the sporadic skirmishes and winter storms, Melián's crews were able to recover more than 380 silver ingots, 67,000 silver coins, and eight bronze cannons from the *Margarita*. Surveys failed to locate any more of the *Atocha*'s cargo.

The treasure which had brought so little luck to the people aboard the *Margarita* brought mixed blessings to Melián. Jealous political rivals complained that Melián had misappropriated some of the salvaged treasure. However, the Council of the Indies declined to act on the charges and he was appointed governor of Venezuela. His appointment was conditional on finding someone to work the *Margarita* site. Melián hired Captain Juan de Anuez, who continued the salvage on and off until 1641. Hearing that the Indians of the Keys knew where the *Atocha* lay, Melián applied for another salvage contract in that year. But, before anything was found, Melián died in 1644. His salvage accounts were audited in Havana and the documents eventually forwarded to Seville, Spain to join the other commercial documents in the Archives of the Indies.

Throughout the rest of the 17th century, Spain's fortunes spiraled downward as the English, French, and Dutch attacked her both in Europe and overseas. In the Americas the strategically-located Turks and Caicos Islands, which straddle one of only two deep water approaches to the vital Windward Passage between Hispaniola and Cuba, fell to the English. So did Bermuda and Jamaica. The Dutch took Curaçao and St. Maarten. The French moved into Hispaniola, naming half of it "Haiti," and into the lower Antilles—Guadeloupe, Martinique,

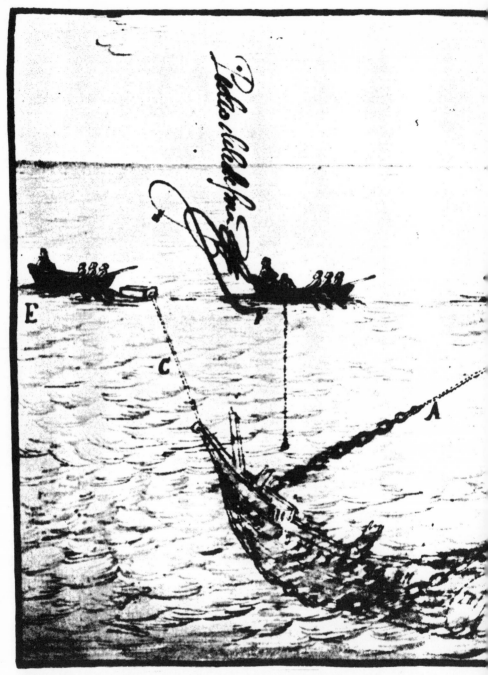

The Spanish were tireless and ingenius salvors. When a treasure ship was lost, they were usually the first to salvage it. Using divers and other methods, they were often able to recover a large portion of the ship's cargo. This period drawing shows one search technique used to search for the Margarita and the Atocha in 1623. Two frigates under full sail drag a chain (D) 350 to 400 feet long.

A wooden buoy (C) showed the exact center of the chain, so that it could be kept spread open in a wide semicircle. Two rowboats (F and G) measured the depth of the water with sounding leads. When the chain snagged something, the rowboats let down grappling hooks to determine whether they had found a ship or a natural obstruction, such as a rock.

Grenada. Captain Henry Morgan began the notorious piracies that made him a legend in England and hated throughout the Spanish empire. Morgan sacked Portobello and Panama City in Panama, and Maracaibo, Venezuela. The Caribbean was no longer a "Spanish Lake."

In 1688, the *Casa de Contrastacion* tallied the sunken vessels still missing; the *Atocha* was at the top of the list. Hurricanes and pirates continued to take their toll on other treasure ships. In 1715 and 1733 entire fleets were lost off the Florida coast. The Spanish salvaged what they could from these wrecks, too, although they were continually harried by the English pressing down from Virginia, the Carolinas, and Nassau in the Bahamas. In 1817 a new power, the United States, bought Florida, transforming it from a strategic military outpost between Spain and her New World colonies into a thinly-populated agricultural backwater. The legacy of Imperial Spain was forgotten, and the records locating the treasure wrecks were moved to Seville.

chapter 3

The Search Begins

The wrecks of the Spanish treasure fleets, and the records of them, remained undisturbed for centuries. In 1960, shipwreck historian John S. Potter Jr. published a book, *The Treasure Diver's Guide* which listed many rich Spanish wrecks and their presumed locations. Soon a small fraternity of ambitious men were combing the shallow coastal waters of Florida. The Spanish wrecks weren't totally unknown. Art McKee, a salvage diver who lived in Key Largo, just south of Miami, had been raising galleon cannons and anchors since the 1930s. A building contractor named Kip Wagner had followed a trail of silver *reales* from a beach near Sebastian Inlet out into the breakers. Wagner took up scuba diving, and by the early 1960s had discovered the remains of one of the 1715 ships. Wagner and other treasure hunters formed a company, Real 8, to excavate the 1715 fleet.

In 1962, one of the Real 8 partners visited a California treasure hunter named Mel Fisher. Mel had given up chicken farming to try his hand at treasure hunting. After several shipwreck expeditions to the Caribbean he was interested in learning about what was going on in Florida. The news of Spanish treasure in shallow waters convinced Fisher to join Real 8. He moved to Florida, bringing with him his wife, Dolores, and a group that included Demothenes "Mo-mo" Molinar, Dick Williams, Rupert Gates, Walt Holzman, and Fay Feild. Dolores, nicknamed "Deo" was an accomplished diver and an integral part of Mel's salvage plans. Molinar was a diesel mechanic and diver from Panama. Rupert Gates was a cartographer. Dick Williams was a mechanic and welder from Texas, and Walt Holzworth had worked with Mel on a previous expedition. Feild, an electronics wizard, had designed Fisher's secret weapon in the search for treasure. Like Melián's copper diving bell, it was an existing technology being adapted to a new use.

Feild's device was an improved version of the flux-gate magnetometer. The Earth's magnetic field is fairly constant except where it is disturbed by the presence of a large magnetic object. When towed in the water, the magnetometer measures variations in the magnetic field and is therefore able to detect things made of magnetic metals, such as iron or steel. During World War II, the Navy used magnetometers to find submarines. Feild and Fisher hoped to use theirs to find galleon anchors and cannons marking the site of treasure wrecks.

Fisher's group soon found wrecks. But they also found that the 1715 ships had sunk very close to shore, where the water is turbulent and silty. Mel was up to the challenge, however. With Fay Feild's help, he designed an elbow-shaped metal duct, which they called a "mailbox," that fit over a boat's propeller. Mel's idea was to push clear water from the surface down to the murky bottom. The first time they tried it, sure enough, a huge bubble of clear water slowly inched down to the bottom, vastly improving the diver's ability to see the wreck they were working. And it had another important effect—the force of the propwash being directed down blew sand off of the wreck. In one stroke, they'd figured out how to improve visibility on the bottom and remove the vast amounts of sand that covered the wrecksites.

The treasure found by Real 8 and Fisher's group inflamed the imagination of the world. A widely publicized auction of artifacts—including a magnificent dragon-shaped gold whistle belonging to Don Juan Esteban de Ubilla, commander of the 1715 fleet—was mounted by New York's Parke Bernet Galleries.

Collectors weren't the only ones interested in the treasure wrecks. By 1967, the State of Florida placed all wrecks in state waters under the jurisdiction of its Department of State. A state archaeologist was hired. Anyone searching in state waters was required to apply for a salvage contract specifying the search area and agreeing that 25% of all finds would be given to the state. Over the next decade, this law would become the centerpiece of a vicious three-way legal battle between the United States Federal Government, the State of Florida, and Mel Fisher. The stakes: ownership of a half-billion dollars worth of treasure and the right of private citizens to search for and dive on historic shipwrecks.

As the 1960s ended, the salvage of the 1715 and 1733 ships was completed. The small, tight-knit—and fractious—fraternity of treasure hunters soon turned back to Potter's book for new targets. At the head of their list—as it had been at the head of the *Casa de Contrastacion's* 1688 list—was the *Atocha*. Potter, perhaps relying on Bartolome Lopez' sighting of the *Atocha* "near the last Key of Matecumbe," reported that the wreck was off Alligator Reef near Matecumbe Key. Matecumbe is in the Middle Keys, halfway between Key West and Key Largo.

old Bullion

Working alone, a diver uses a small hand-held blower to remove sand and shells in the search for more artifacts.

More than 200 pounds of gold were listed on the Atocha's manifest. Unlike silver, which quickly corrodes in sea water, gold retains its luster even after centuries in the ocean.

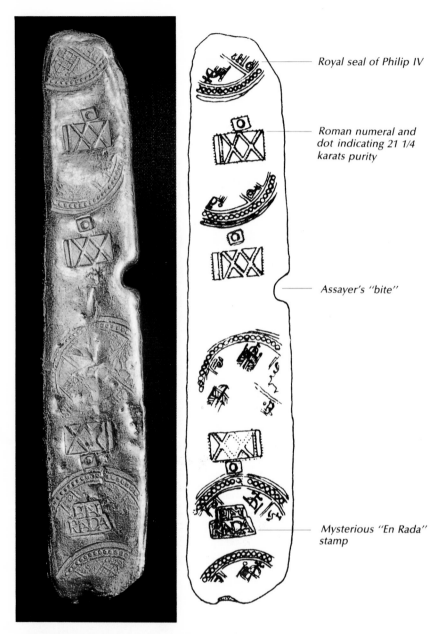

Royal seal of Philip IV

Roman numeral and dot indicating 21 1/4 karats purity

Assayer's "bite"

Mysterious "En Rada" stamp

In September 1974, the Quicksands area yielded this one pound, five-ounce gold bar. Like all other precious metals leaving the New World, gold bars were meticulously marked with stamps and seals noting the purity of the bars, the mint where they were cast, and whether the King's tax had been paid. Gold bars shipped legally show an assayer's "bite," a gouge where a small piece of the bar has been taken to test its purity. This bar bears the cryptic legend "En Rada," which has not yet been deciphered. It is just one more of the mysteries posed by the treasures of the Atocha.

Unlike the silver bars on the Atocha's manifest, the gold bars were not individually listed as clearly, making it more difficult to use them in identifying the wreck. The small bars are often called "finger bars" due to their size

Treasure doesn't always come in big amounts; this diver was rewarded for hours of underwater search by the discovery of this tiny piece of a gold bar. While it seems hard to believe a wrecksite marked by 50 tons of precious metals, 20 cannons, six anchors, and 200 tons of rock ballast could elude searchers for 16 years, this tiny artifact sums up the problem: it's a big ocean, and even a galleon is a small object in such vast unexplored expanses.

This gold disc weighing almost five pounds bears marks showing its purity, 15¾ karats, and tax stamps.

Not all of the bullion shipped on the galleons was properly taxed. Even though the penalty for smuggling untaxed gold was severe—200 lashes and ten years chained to the oar of a Spanish galley— contraband bullion often amounts to 20% of the weight of the legal bullion listed on a ship's manifest. In the case of the Margarita, divers have already recovered more gold than was listed on the ship's manifest, most of it untaxed contraband. These bits, from gold bars are obviously not contraband because they bear the royal tax seal.

The *Atocha* had eluded Spanish salvors for nearly a half-century. Now, although a number of groups searched for it, the *Atocha* still couldn't be found. The treasure hunters who'd had such quick success with the 1715 fleet were baffled. Extensive magnetometer surveys and test digs turned up plenty of iron cannons and anchors but no copper, no silver ingots, no *Atocha*. The ship soon acquired an almost mythic status. With the *Santa Margarita*, it became known as one of the Ghost Galleons of 1622.

With hopes of locating the elusive *Atocha* and *Santa Margarita*, whose treasures exceeded $500 million, Mel Fisher joined the search in the Middle Keys. Unsuccessful open water searches using the magnetometer took Treasure Salvors on an 85-mile search of the Florida Keys from Marathon on Matecumbe Key to Key Largo, the northernmost Key, and back. Still they found no sign of the 1622 shipwreck. Mel wondered how his troupe of divers could be missing the seemingly well-documented treasure. Lopez' statement to the Marquis of Cadereita was clear enough, placing the wreck near Matecumbe. Adding to the confusion, an English narrative located the lost galleons "in the place of the Cabeza de los Martires in Matecumbe." *Cabeza* meant "head" and *martires* meant "martyrs," yet another Spanish name for the Florida Keys. The English version seemed to place the wreck at the "head of the Keys," which meant Key Largo.

Mel wasn't the only salvor baffled by the elusive treasure. Continental Exploration, a salvage company formed by Art McKee, Burt Webber, and Jack Haskins was looking for the *Atocha* as well. McKee was by now known as the grandfather of Spanish shipwreck salvage in Florida. Burt Webber, his protege, would later win fame by finding the *Nuestra Señora de la Concepcion*, a rich galleon sunk in the Caribbean. Haskins, a self-taught historian, was able to read the often-confusing Spanish accounts of the fleet's loss. They had copies of documents from the Archive of the Indies in Seville, Spain, which they believed showed conclusively that the 1622 fleet was lost near Matecumbe Key.

The Archive of the Indies is home to thousands of bundles of documents representing millions of pages of testimony to Spain's historical heritage in the New World. Early Spanish documents are written in a language very similar to today's modern dialect. Theoretically, almost anyone fluent in Spanish should be able to decipher these documents without too much difficulty. But in practice it's a different story. The writing style is a flowing script called *procesal*—rounded characters joined by unbroken chains of Arabic-like letters. Even the trained eye has difficulty translating the illegible scrawl.

To make matters worse, there's very little punctuation in early Spanish writing. Translators must learn to structure sentences from long, continuous text filled with numerous archaic abbreviations. And though well preserved, the ink and paper have faded with time, are riddled with worm holes or are badly torn.

The documents are tied into bundles called *legajos*, and are housed in 14 different sections within the Archive. An individual bundle may contain thousands of handwritten documents which may not even relate to one another. There are 26 huge volumes and a number of smaller ledgers that index a tiny fraction of the more than 50 million items on file. But, usually the only way to learn what information a particular *legajo* might contain is to wade through it page by page.

Mel knew that his competitors had documents from the Archive relating to the 1622 fleet. He decided to visit Seville to research the galleons. As Mel and his wife and partner, Deo, wandered through the repository, it became apparent that the valuable clues to the *Atocha's* whereabouts were beyond their expertise. How were they to find out anything about the *Atocha* when they couldn't read Spanish and couldn't find their way through the disorganized documents? Señora Angeles Flores, a Spanish researcher, had helped others with research on the 1622 fleet and agreed to help Mel. But Mel knew they needed another researcher who could dig deeper into the records for new clues.

About the same time, Eugene Lyon, a graduate student of Latin American History at the University of Florida, was on his way to Seville to continue research for his doctoral dissertation on Florida's Spanish origins. Mel and Gene got to know each other when both joined a new Methodist church near their homes in Vero Beach, Florida. While working on his dissertation, Gene had become familiar with the Archive, and learned to quickly scan barely legible documents for important key words or phrases. He had already come across several documents relating to the *Atocha*, and found the cargo manifests for both the *Atocha* and *Margarita*. The closer these documents pulled him to these historical vessels, the more Gene became interested in unveiling the whole mosaic of the Indies trade to the Americas.

Mel and Deo knew they badly needed Gene's expertise. Before they returned to Florida they hired Gene as a consultant. Just ten days after the Fisher's visit, Gene found the accounts of Francisco Nunez Melián's salvage efforts on the *Santa Margarita*. Lyon labored over the rolling *procesal* script. The many references to *Cayos de Mate- cumbe* seemed to confirm Potter's assertion that the *Atocha* and *Santa Margarita* went down near Matecumbe Key. But then Lyon stumbled across a new piece of evidence: According to the account, Melián had found the shipwreck in the *Cayos del Marques*—Spanish for the Keys of the Marquis. Lyon learned from other research that the Marquis of Cadereita had taken charge of the salvage efforts in 1623, and guessed that the nearby island the Spanish had camped on had been named for the Marquis. But where did this island lie today?

Two historical maps of Florida—one each from the 17th and 18th centuries—soon completed the puzzle. The 17th century map showed a group of islands to the east of the Tortugas labeled *Marquez*. The 18th century map provided more vital information: the same group of islands was labeled *Cayos del Marquez*. Apparently, the term Matecumbe had been generic for all the islands along the southern tip of Florida. Over the years they had been renamed, one by one, until today only two islands—Upper Matecumbe Key and Lower Matecumbe Key—still bear the original group name. To Lyon, this meant that the wreck should be located near the present-day Marquesas Keys, about 20 miles west of Key West and a little over 40 miles from Fort Jefferson National Monument in the Dry Tortugas.

"It was easy for researchers to pass over the small bit of information," Lyon explains in his book, *The Search For The Atocha*, published in 1979 by Harper & Row. "In their research, Mel, Burt Webber, and Bob Marx (a shipwreck salvor) had concentrated on documents written at the time of the fleet disaster or shortly thereafter. However, as a result of the first salvage operations, one of the *Matecumbes* had been renamed, but only documents generated after that time bore the new name. The modern salvors had leaped to the conclusion that the 1622 shipwrecks were near the modern Matecumbe Keys. Actually, they had been off by more than 100 miles."

Another reason they all were so far off the trail of the *Atocha* was that Señora Angeles Flores, though an able researcher, didn't understand the geography of the Keys. With the help of Gene Lyon, Mel was the first salvor to catch the oversight. But he, too, would eventually be misguided by Angeles Flores' unfamiliarity with the geography of the Florida Keys.

By the summer of 1970, Fisher had withdrawn his search contract in the Middle Keys and moved the company to new headquarters in Key West. Still, the exact location of the 1622 shipwreck was unknown, and Lyon directed Treasure Salvors to search the waters surrounding the Marquesas Keys. The search area stretched from Half Moon Shoals eastward to Sand Key near Key West—a slice of trackless ocean almost 50 miles long and nearly five miles wide.

From a starting point ten miles west of the Marquesas, Mel's search boat, *Holly's Folly*, captained and owned by Bob Holloway, burned 200 gallons of fuel a day as it moved slowly eastward, dragging the magnetometer over mile after mile of shallow bottom. There were plenty of "hits" with the magnetometer—readings that showed metal below. One by one they were checked out, turning up nothing of value.

By early fall, Mel's search efforts still hadn't produced results. In September, Gene, back home in Vero Beach, received new information from Angeles Flores. Flores wrote that an eyewitness account of the sinking of the *Santa Margarita* stated that the ship went down east of the islands. Captain de Lugo's eyewitness account also showed that the *Atocha* had gone down three miles further east of the *Margarita*. This

new information from Flores seemed to suggest that Treasure Salvors
had been searching on the wrong side of the Marquesas!

By January 1971, the 34-foot *Holly's Folly* had thoroughly
combed the Boca Grande Channel east of the Marquesas. The only
wreck they'd found was that of a World War II aircraft. Angeles Flores,
who was still researching the 1622 shipwreck in Seville, had sent copies
of the documents she'd found to Gene Lyon. Perhaps these would turn
up a new clue. Sure enough, the accounts of the *Santa Margarita* wreck
provided new information, but not exactly the kind that would please
Mel's crew of frustrated divers. Angeles Flores had made a mistake in
translating the documents. When Gene examined the originals, he
found that the *Margarita* sank *veste del ultimo cavo*—*west* of the "last key."
The treasure hunters had been correct when they started west of the
Marquesas, and now they actually had been searching the wrong side of
the Marquesas for four months.

It was an unfortunate—and expensive—oversight. To date,
Treasure Salvors had invested more than $200,000 in their search for the
1622 galleons. If Mel was to continue the exploration, he would need
more money. But to attract more investors, Fisher needed some proof
that the investment would pay off—he needed a piece of the *Atocha*.

And he got it. Or something that he thought resembled it,
anyway. On June 12, 1971, the monotonous days of dragging the
magnetometer back and forth in the blazing subtropical sun paid off.
Bob Holloway, and the crew of *Holly's Folly* recorded a large "double
peg" reading on their magnetometers indicating a big piece of iron. As
usual, a buoy was thrown overboard while the crew dragged on their
scuba gear to check it out. This time, it wasn't a fish trap and it wasn't a
lost Navy airplane. It was a galleon anchor!

Everyone except Mel was uncertain of its significance. He
donned his diving gear and plunged into the warm water. Almost
immediately he came up with the evidence he had waited for for more
than four years—one small lead musketball. This was all the proof Mel
needed. He knew that he had discovered the lost remains of the *Atocha*
or the *Margarita*.

A few days later, Don Kincaid, a professional underwater photographer aboard the *Virgilona*, was preparing to dive on the anchor. Don
had met Mel a few months earlier and was now on a freelance assignment
to photograph the galleon anchor. Don descended through a cloud of sand
and swam into the crater where the anchor was exposed. Suddenly he saw
the brilliant links of an 8½-foot gold chain. Treasure Salvors' newest ac-
quaintance, who later became a company vice-president and a member
of its Board of Directors, had found the first piece of gold. Aboard the *Virgilona*, Mel uncorked a bottle of champagne to celebrate the find. "To the
Atocha," he toasted. "Here's to the rest of all that loot—that $400 million—
right down here. It's real close now. I can smell it."

Almost immediately, Fisher applied for a salvage contract on the site. The *Virgilona* crew continued its exploratory digging and quickly uncovered more artifacts: encrusted matchlock muskets, iron cannonballs, some iron barrel hoops, and ballast stones. Though significant finds, in the sense that the style of the weapons suggested that the crew had located an early 17th century Spanish military vessel, there was still no concrete evidence that these were remains of the *Atocha* or *Margarita*. Even the two six-inch gold bars recovered on October 23 couldn't unlock the mystery. Although they bore markings, none of them had inscriptions which could be compared to the ships' manifests. The only conclusion the divers could draw was that the gold bars were untaxed, unregistered contraband being smuggled back to Spain.

The success of the early summer soon paled, and the next nine months would sorely test Mel's optimism and the staff's commitment. Again and again, Mel told his divers, "Today's the day," an expression that became the crew's credo. Though the young divers shared an intense camaraderie, the uncertainty grew through 1972. At the end of each long day of diving—sometimes midnight—they still hadn't found conclusive evidence that this was the site of the *Atocha* or *Santa Margarita*. The only substantial find of that year was the wreck of an English vessel dated about 1700. Gene's documents on the early Spanish salvage attempts suggested that Mel was diving in the right spot, but the infrequent finds suggested otherwise.

In the meantime, Fisher's competitors had abandoned their search for the 1622 galleons in the Middle Keys and turned their attention to the Marquesas. Jack Haskins and another researcher, John Berrier, flew to Seville to search the Archive of the Indies. Ironically, they sat just a few feet from Gene Lyon, who had returned to Seville to continue his research for Mel. For weeks the three men carefully studied accounts of the early salvage efforts for some clue as to the location of the vast treasure. It became clear to Gene that the race for the *Atocha* and *Santa Margarita* was on. "Neither [Haskins nor Berrier] believed that Mel had found it yet," Lyon recalled. "Once, we called for the same bundle at the same time—in an archive with 40,000 bundles of paper, the odds against that are considerable."

Perhaps the entry of Haskins and Berrier, and their colleagues Burt Webber and Richard MacAllaster, into the race for the *Atocha* was just the pressure Treasure Salvors needed to continue its search. After all, there were plenty of reasons to abandon the project. Mel was again in desperate need of financing, particularly since he was suddenly ordered to pay $250,000 to a former partner in suit that had been in litigation in California for seven years.

But more troublesome was the difficulty between Treasure Salvors and the State of Florida. Fisher had already received a stiff warning from Florida's marine archaeologist, Carl Clausen. There were many prob-

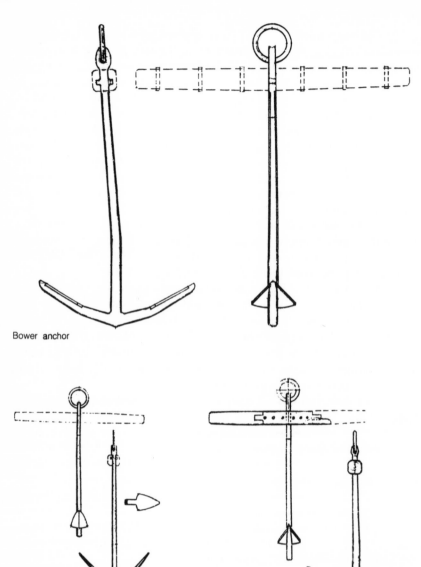

Bower anchor

Kedge anchor

Stream anchor

Strict rules specified the number and type of anchors to be carried aboard the Spanish ships to be trading in the New World. The Atocha construction contract called for six anchors, each of a specific size. The Margarita carried the same number and types of anchors.

To date, ten anchors have been found on the site. This constitutes the largest collection of closely dated galleon anchors from an archaeological site in the New World. Comparative studies of these anchors are giving scholars new insights into the evolution of ground tackle from the time of Columbus to the Napoleonic period.

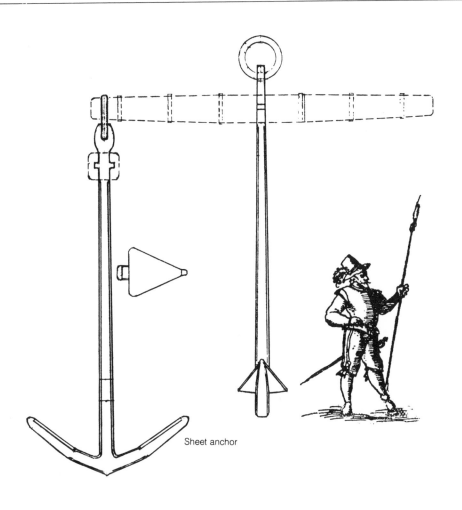

Sheet anchor

Bower anchors were a ship's primary anchors. Each ship carried two, one on the starboard and one on the port bow. This is one of the Margarita anchors found during a magnetometer search inside the Outer Reef. It was probably hooked into the reef in a last ditch attempt to keep the ship from being pushed up into the shallow Quicksands. Note the bent shank, Spanish anchors were known to be badly made.

The only cast iron anchor yet found on the sites, this kedging anchor was located near the Margarita bower anchor. On its crown are several well-preserved inscriptions: the date, 1618, and a foundry mark.

A stream anchor from the Margarita was found with a well-preserved wooden stock. An analysis by Forest Products Laboratories of the U.S. Department of Agriculture showed that it was made of three kinds of wood: rosewood, a type of palm, and a wood known as ipe or lapacho.

The sheet anchor, such as this one from the Atocha, was the largest anchor on the ship. The sheet anchor was usually carried in the hold with its wooden stocks removed and was used only in dire emergencies. This anchor, the first large piece of the 1622 ships located, was found in the Quicksands in 1971. The figure drawn to scale with the rest of the anchors represents about 5½ feet. This is to show the actual size of the sheet anchor.

lems with the state. A memorandum written in January 1972 by Alan W. Dorian, one of the state's field archaeology agents, lists a number of alleged accidents and poor working conditions during Treasure Salvors' expeditions, as well as contract violations. Between June and October 1971, Dorian noted nine accidents or injuries and seven contract violations. "Undoubtedly, more have occurred," Dorian wrote. "I am recommending that an in-depth investigation of possible contractual violations be made and that positive demonstrable action be taken by Mr. Fisher and this Division to vastly improve the physical condition of all vessels, machinery, and equipment involved in this contract."

State agents and Mel's adversaries also openly questioned the authenticity of recent finds. Carl Clausen's successor Wilburn A. (Sonny) Cockrell was highly suspicious about the two gold bars. Bob Marx claimed that Mel had stolen the anchor from a shipwreck salvaged earlier by Marx.

Though the allegations would continue for years, for Treasure Salvors, the summer of 1973 would end years of uncertainty and frustration, and be the start of a dream that Fisher and his 20 crewmen had long awaited. The list of artifacts recovered during May and June was encouraging: nearly 4,000 silver pieces-of-four and-eight, muskets, swords, daggers, a pair of scissors, bar shot, a lock and key, potsherds, barrel hoops and—perhaps the most prized possession—a pilot's astrolabe, one of less than two dozen known to exist in the world, found by Mel's son Dirk, Captain of the tugboat *Northwind*.

Kim Fisher's *Southwind* crew located gold—a long gold bar minus official markings, a 15 ¼-karat gold disk bearing royal seals and an assayers mark, and two gold coins stamped with the symbol of the Seville mint.

Despite these finds, the suspicion and harassment continued. The Florida Department of State was given an anonymous tip that Treasure Salvors had failed to pay its corporate tax and, therefore, should have its salvage contract cancelled. Treasure Salvors received an official apology from the state when it produced a copy of the receipt showing it had paid the tax. A similar episode occurred concerning licensing of Treasure Salvors' tugboats. When the documents were produced, state officials backed off. Mel was also charged with failure to keep adequate maps of the holes dug by the boats; failure to operate the mailboxes at proper speed at all times; and removing artifacts from the wrecksite without the authorization of state field agents.

Bleth McHaley, who had been working with Mel for several years in the Treasure Salvors office, was very concerned by the troubles with the state and the negative stories appearing in the media. She knew the power of the press. Originally from Minnesota, Bleth had kicked around the world for a time before settling in California, where she worked for *Skin Diver Magazine*, a publication about scuba diving. She met Mel at his Redondo Beach dive shop in the 1950s, and in 1971 agreed to join Treasure Salvors as director of public affairs.

Now, with the state breathing down their necks and unfavorable reports appearing regularly in the *Miami Herald*, one of the state's most influential newspapers, Bleth together with Don Kincaid and Gene Lyon convinced Mel that if he was to continue to attract investors, and avoid any more trouble with the state that could jeopardize future salvage contract requests, the company needed some credibility. It needed a professional archaeologist.

PART
II

"If you can really utilize the manifest, you are going to know a whole
culture. Not just bar silver, not just gold pieces that are identifiable
on the registry, not silverware...but the whole economic, governmental,
financial system of the Spanish Empire. You're talking about the
marine technology and the culture that these people inherited from
the Phoenecians, the Greeks, the Romans, and the Portuguese...
But until you know how to read a registry, you cannot know what is
in it. Until you understand the empire that stood in back of it, the
officers and men who administered it, the jealousies in the fleet
system, and the problems between the merchants and the fleet generals,
you can't talk about the cargo of a ship."

Dr. Eugene Lyon,
Research Historian
Treasure Salvors Inc.

chapter 4

Archaeological Challenge

une 15, 1973
I have discovered the remains of two 17th century shipwrecks. One is English and one is Spanish. I need an archaeologist. Gene Lyon has told me of your interest in pottery. We have loads of it for you to study. I am sending you a round trip ticket. Call if you are interested in coming to Key West.

Mel Fisher, President
Treasure Salvors, Inc.

When this telegram reached me in Jamaica, it took me completely by surprise. I had never met Mel Fisher, had never been to Key West. I wasn't even a certified diver, much less a marine archaeologist. I knew Mel's researcher, Gene Lyon. Several years before, Gene had given me some Spanish documents that helped me interpret a Spanish land site I was working in Jamaica.

Since 1960, I had lived abroad; first as a graduate student in Britain, then as a government archaeologist in Ghana, West Africa. In 1970, I moved to Jamaica to help excavate Spanish colonial land sites of the 16th and 17th centuries.

As I read the telegram a second and third time, my head spun. My wife, Marie, and I had already decided to leave Jamaica in the next few months. However, we had no idea of where we would go or what we would do. Marie had just received her Ph.D in anthropology and had sent out a few feelers for jobs in the United States, but had received little response. For over a year, I had been sending job inquiries to the U.S. Department of Interior's National Park Service and to the State of Florida. But finding work as an archaeologist is tough under the best of conditions and I knew I had several things going against me.

Although I had completed four years of graduate studies toward my Ph.D in archaeology at the University of Edinburgh in Scotland and at the Institute of Archaeology at the University of London, I had gotten wanderlust before completing my dissertation. I had become a research fellow, doing exciting archaeology in the West African bush and had lost all enthusiasm for the paperwork I needed to finish before receiving my degree. Now, after working as a professional archaeologist for a decade, the only paper credentials I had was a Bachelor of Arts degree in geology with a minor in anthropology from Dartmouth College.

The lack of a formal post-graduate degree hadn't hampered my work in West Africa or for the Institute of Jamaica in Kingston. However, I soon found it was going to be a major barrier to getting work in the U.S. In 1972, I attended my first archaeological conference in the U.S. It was traumatic. Having been trained overseas, I was a total outsider. I didn't have a recognized post-graduate degree and I didn't have an influential American archaeologist as a mentor. Without these, I was unable to tap into the network that academics acquire during their graduate school days. I knew then it was going to be terribly difficult to break into the tight, close-knit community of archaeologists in the U.S. I came away from that conference knowing it was going to be hard to "come home." I had no idea how hard it was actually going to be.

I attended another conference in 1972, the annual meeting of the Florida Historical Society. It was there that I first met Gene Lyon. We had been corresponding for about a year, and his letters and documents had given my Jamaican research a tremendous boost. Gene and I talked about his work with Mel Fisher, and slowly, the whole tantalizing story of the *Atocha* began to unfold. As a result of my work in Jamaica, I considered myself pretty familiar with the archaeology of the period, but much of what Gene had to say astonished me. I had already studied artifacts recovered from the sea—I had worked with material salvaged from Port Royal, the Jamaican pirate capital that had sunk into Kingston Harbor during an earthquake in 1692. As Gene talked, I began to see shipwrecks as the best outlet for the kind of research I wanted to pursue.

After the meeting, Gene told Mel about my interest in Spanish colonial archaeology. Mel's telegram was an invitation to join the hunt. My professional life had been unconventional so far, and I had a feeling things were about to take an even more bizarre twist. I was about to risk what little credibility I might be able to claim with academic archaeologists in the U.S. by signing on with a treasure hunter—and one who was not particularly popular at that.

While he'd succeeded in finding and identifying—at least to his own satisfaction—the site of the *Atocha*, Mel still faced serious challenges on several fronts. The state continued its legal actions against

Mel, claiming that it owned the wrecksite. At the same time, state archaeologists asserted that Treasure Salvors wasn't living up to the state's standards for research carried out on a shipwreck. Treasure Salvors' records of artifacts found, digging procedures, and mapping were heavily criticized by the state officials.

This wasn't entirely Mel's fault. The state contract specified that state field archaeological agents were to be present at all times site work was done. Though these agents—mostly young archaeology students with scant experience in historic shipwreck salvage—were present at all times, they were inexperienced. They had made little progress in either giving direction to the work being done on the site or in understanding the significance of the various artifacts as they were uncovered.

Senator Robert Williams, who supervised the state's shipwreck salvage program, seemed to favor Continental Explorations, the group that included Haskins, Webber, and MacAllaster, in its recommendations on salvage contracts. Bleth McHaley felt that the addition of a professional archaeologist to the staff would help defend Treasure Salvors against the state's criticisms.

There was another important reason to hire an experienced archaeologist: investment capital. A continuing flow of money from investors was crucial to the survival of the company. New artifacts coming up from the bottom would help maintain their confidence in the project. Though the crew had recovered several rare and unique artifacts, it had yet to find the main bulk of the treasure cargo. It was now apparent that the wreck had broken up either during the sinking or shortly afterward, and the wreckage was strewn over an enormous area. It would take a disciplined, highly organized effort, meticulous record keeping, and innovative archaeological techniques to find the rest of the ship, with its thousand silver ingots and quarter-million coins.

To me, the *Atocha* and the *Margarita* were the main characters of a first-rate mystery story. After spending nearly 15 years working archaeological sites on land, shipwreck archaeology seemed the ultimate challenge. It is basically the process of reconstructing both an event—a sinking—and the lifestyle of the passengers and crew using almost non-existent physical evidence.

It's as though Arthur Conan Doyle had set for Sherlock Holmes the task of solving a murder 350 years after the crime was committed. Holmes would face the same difficulties facing Mel: The eyewitnesses are dead. The scene of the crime has first to be located from incomplete records before it can be examined for clues. Scanty knowledge of the most trivial everyday affairs, such as where the sailmaker might have kept his tools, made every assumption, every theory, a stretch beyond known facts into the realm of thinly-supported supposition. How could I apply the careful scientific techniques learned on land to a shipwreck scattered over miles of sand that was stirred and churned by every passing storm?

Not everyone believed that good archaeology could be done on such a wreck. Popular writers have sometimes described shipwrecks as being mute testimonies from the past. Nothing could be further from the truth. Shipwrecks, like any other archaeological site, are only silent to those who don't know how to interpret the artifacts. Once archaeologists learn how to ask questions in the right way, the seemingly unrelated artifacts begin to fit together, like a jig-saw puzzle, into a coherent picture.

The objects begin to reveal where and how they were made and how they may have been used on board a particular ship. These individual stories tell much about the ships themselves and the men who sailed in them. By linking the stories together, archaeologists can assemble a cultural mosaic about life at sea that can't be gotten from documents alone. Those who were best equipped to tell us that story, the people who sailed on the early voyages of discovery, often failed to record specific details about life at sea: Where did the officers, crew, and passengers eat? Where did they sleep? How did the passengers spend the long days below decks? With these details, history can be easily understood even by people who have little or no real feeling for the past.

Without a full written record of the lifestyles and history of the times, archaeologists must learn to piece together this information from the fragments and remains of the ship, most of which are encrusted with coral or disguised by heavy corrosion.

Despite the fact that the *Atocha* had broken up and her artifacts were scattered and deteriorated, the 1622 galleon was still a fabulous archaeological site. Unlike sites on land, a shipwreck is an almost perfect snapshot of a given moment in history. Cities change over the years. Buildings are put up and torn down, and the character of an area's population changes. However, at the instant a ship goes down, it becomes a time capsule, entombing both the people on board and the tools and possessions that exemplify their way of life. Thus, shipwreck archaeology can fill in important details erased from dry land sites by the passage of time.

The study of artifacts from the *Atocha* and the *Margarita* would help recreate the fascinating details of America's Spanish history—one that began over a century before the Pilgrims landed at Plymouth Rock. The largest collection of Spanish artifacts in America is not to be found in museums, but instead in the numerous shipwrecks that still lie undiscovered throughout the Caribbean Basin and along the southern shores of the United States.

The *Atocha* site was a way for me to prove that real archaeology could be done on a shallow water wreck with as much certainty as on a deep water wreck or dry land. In 1973, there were very few professional archaeologists who believed that. In interpreting the meaning of artifacts, whether from a land site or a shipwreck, it's important to know the spatial relationship between the locations of various artifacts on the site. That's why careful measurements are taken before and during excavations, and why detailed site maps marking the locations of major finds are prepared. Some marine archaeologists and treasure hunters have argued that ships driven onto shallow shoals hit with such force that spatial relationships between artifacts on board are destroyed. In a report of his work on a wreck from the 1715 treasure fleet, Carl Clausen, the first marine archaeologist for the State of Florida, had written that the jumbled and scattered artifacts showed no discernible spatial relationship. I had studied Clausen's report and his site map. Instead of a hopeless and confused jumble, I could see definite clusters of gold and silver artifacts which suggested a rudimentary patterning of artifacts.

Of course, the shifting of material during the sinking and disintegration of the vessel make it almost impossible to determine precise spatial relationships between artifacts. However, clusters of artifacts on a site can indicate the part of the vessel that's being excavated. Their pattern on the bottom can reveal the sequence of events that lead up to and followed the sinking. In the case of the *Atocha*, the failure to find the main hull in the immediate vicinity of the anchor made this kind of interpretation a practical necessity if the bulk of the site's artifacts—and Mel's treasure—were to be found.

From my experiences at U.S. archaeological conferences, I knew that accepting Mel's offer to work as the group's archaeologist also meant volunteering to have myself run through a buzzsaw of professional opposition. Not only would I be flaunting the conventional wisdom about shallow water shipwrecks, but working with treasure hunters as well.

Archaeology is a young science. It is really only in this century that it has been accepted by the larger scientific establishment as something other than grave robbing and pot hunting. For years, archaeology was considered a hobby for ghoulish amateurs, and many of the most important finds were those linked to burial sites, such as the tombs of the Egyptian Pharaohs. Some members of more established branches of science (such as astronomy, which has tradition stretching back into pre-history), thought of archaeologists as late-comers more interested in finding gold and silver trinkets than in knowledge.

Academic archaeologists are therefore very sensitive about any association with a profit-making commercial venture. "Proper" excavations are those funded by museums, universities, and non-profit organizations. Unfortunately, in the case of shipwrecks, this means that the number of wrecks excavated will be very, very small. To date, few universities or museums have funded the excavation of colonial period Spanish shipwrecks in the Americas. The wrecks excavated to date have almost all been worked by commercial salvors. Still, there are vast

Gold Cup and Plate

Wealthy persons returning to Spain carried their valuables with them, and many personal possessions of great value have been recovered. The exquisite detail of this gold plate, found on the Margarita site by Dick Klaudt in the summer of 1980, illustrates the quality of craftsmanship of the goldsmiths of the era.

This crushed "Poison Cup," found by Kim Fisher in 1973, was once ringed inside with precious stones and undoubtedly belonged to a person of high rank. The finely etched cup was called a "poison cup" because the bowl has a cage-type holder for a bezoar stone. The stone was supposedly able to absorb arsenic poison, thus protecting the drinker from being poisoned.

The interior rim of the gold cup is studded with 20 settings which once held brilliant emeralds. The exterior of the cup is decorated with mythical beasts: a phoenix, lion, rabbit, dolphins, and fire-breathing dragons. The dolphins also form the handles of the cup. The lower portion of the bowl is divided into 24 longitudinal sections, each filled with an incised floral design. This cup was restored by Joseph Ternbach working in conjunction with the Queen's Museum in New York.

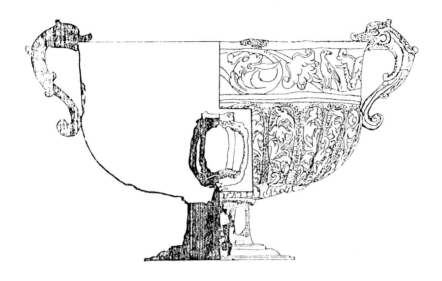

The bezoar stone is an organic concretion derived from the stomach of goats and llamas. It was a Medieval belief that the bezoar would absorb arsenic poison. A number of bezoar stones found on the motherlode site will tell us much about Medieval superstitions and science.

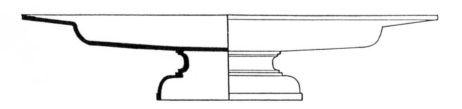

This superbly etched, footed gold plate measures eight inches in diameter and is approximately $\frac{3}{16}$ inch thick. The plate is believed to have been used as a salver. The profile showing the base of the plate was drawn by D. Larissa Dillin.

numbers of shipwrecks that haven't been found. If the knowledge entombed in these wrecks is to be recovered, it will have to be recovered by archaeologists, who have the desire and the scientific skills, working with commercial salvors, who have the capital and the technology to find and excavate the wrecks. Working with Mel would give me a chance to prove that good archaeology coud be done by working *with* the treasure hunters instead of working against them, as the State of Florida had tried to do.

I thought about my meetings with Gene and my feelings about shipwreck archaeology, but I couldn't make a decision about accepting Mel's offer.

A week after the telegram arrived, Bleth McHaley called. She wanted to know whether I would come to Key West to meet Mel. As she described the artifacts that were coming up from the *Atocha* site, there was no mistaking her desire for Treasure Salvors to do good archaeology. She told me how she and Gene had discussed the need to have an archaeologist join the team, and how Mel had quickly supported the idea. I tried to explain to her that I had never excavated an underwater site, much less a galleon crammed full of artifacts. Bleth dismissed my objections and broke in with a description of the mariner's astrolabe they had just found—and in perfect working condition! From the passionate tone of her voice, I could tell that I should be impressed, but at the moment, I wasn't exactly sure what an astrolabe was. As we talked, Bleth pressed me hard for a decision. Bleth can be very persuasive. How could I say no? I told her I would come to Key West to meet Mel.

My first meeting with Mel and his staff is indelibly etched in my mind. As I was flying toward Key West, circumstance was moving just as rapidly to draw me into the search for the *Atocha*. My meeting with Mel was set for July 4, 1973. I arrived at the office early in the morning, expecting to be the center of an interesting, possibly intense meeting. Instead, I found that everyone in the company was waiting for the salvage tug *Southwind* to return to Key West. The *Southwind* was a Mississippi River tugboat that had recently been purchased from Lou Tilley for Treasure Salvors stock. She'd been refitted as a salvage vessel and sent out to the site under the direction of Kim Fisher, Mel's second son. And she'd just struck paydirt.

Just before I arrived, that very morning, diver John Lewis, nicknamed "Bouncy John," donned his diving gear. The first "blow" from the twin mailbox tubes sent a powerful rush of water onto the ocean floor, forming a small crater in the loose sand. Lewis fanned some sand from the shallow crater walls. There, hidden in the side of the crater, was a tiny rosary encrusted with miniature shells. Red coral and gold beads, connected by a gold chain, accented a delicate gold cross.

While Bouncy John was pulling up the rosary, Mel's youngest son, Kane, lowered himself into the water. In a few short minutes, he spotted a piece of evidence that would confirm for the first time the origin of this shipwreck. A long black object lay on the ocean floor—a 60-pound ingot of pure silver. Soon another one turned up, and then a third. The news was radioed back to the Key West office, turning the whole organization upside down. After years of frustration, here was solid evidence that they had found a major Spanish treasure galleon. Everyone was crazy with anticipation, waiting for the ingots to be landed.

Tourists, sightseers, and reporters crowded the decks of the *Golden Doubloon*, Mel's floating office. Champagne corks popped like 4th of July firecrackers as the treasure divers speculated about what the ingots might mean. As I looked at this wild scene unfolding around me, all of the uncertainties I'd had about coming to Key West boiled up in my churning stomach. How had a serious archaeologist like me gotten into the middle of all this? Archaeology was supposed to be done patiently and quietly, in a remote location, holding a small whisk broom. Here I was on the deck of a floating tourist attraction with a virtual circus going on around me. Just then I saw Gene standing to the side, patiently waiting for the *Southwind*. I marveled at his composure. It was clear that he could function as an historian in spite of the chaos around him. Could I do the same?

I tried to talk to Bleth and others in the company, but their attention was riveted on the scales being set up to weigh the silver ingots. In his hands, Gene held a copy of the manifests of the *Atocha* and the *Margarita*. If the silver ingots were from one of those ships, their weights and other markings would be on the manifests.

The *Southwind* pulled in, and the crowd surged forward. Mooring lines were made fast and, at last, the silver was passed over the rail. When Gene Lyon brushed away the silver oxide that darkened the ingots' surface, he revealed marks that showed a tally number, the weight, the fineness of the metal, and the monogram of the merchant who had shipped them. Now they had to be matched to the manifest. First, though, the ingots had to be weighed to determine their exact weights before the other marks were recorded.

It was easy to get caught up in the excitement of the find and drama of confirming the wreck's identity. It took Gene three days to confirm that the silver ingots—numbered 569, 794, and 4584—were cargo of the 1622 galleons. Not finding any of the numbers in the *Margarita* manifest, Gene then went to the *Atocha* manifest where he quickly found the tally number 4584. Mel and Gene were now certain that they had found the *Atocha*. The celebration that week aboard the *Southwind* was a fitting tribute to the crew's dedication and persistence.

Not everyone was eager to celebrate Treasure Salvor's apparent good fortune. Less than two weeks after the find, Burt Webber notified Senator Robert Williams, that two of the silver ingots did not bear the marks listed in his copy of the *Atocha* manifest. As for ingot number 4584, Webber had this to say: "This bar does not carry a mine brand stamping according to the bullion registry. It is my opinion that the number 4584 plus a closeness of weight alone is not enough to make a positive identification. Undoubtedly, there were Spanish treasure galleons before and after the loss of *Atocha* that carried silver bar shipments which could have included bar number 4584."

In closing, Webber concluded he felt sure the artifacts recovered from the 8M0141 location, the state's identification number for the wrecksite, were from an early 17th century Spanish galleon, but not the *Atocha*. "This entire scheme is obviously in the interests of stock promotion and it does surprise me to see the Division tolerate this type of conduct," Webber said.

Two weeks later, in a follow-up letter to Senator Williams, Webber retracted his statements about the silver ingots. Webber had mistakenly looked up the wrong numbers in the registry. Burt had sunk alot of time and money into searching for the *Atocha* himself; it was hard for him to admit that Mel had beaten him to it.

I now became fully aware of the challenge before me. No matter what physical evidence came up from the site, no matter how well it corresponded to the manifest and to the written records left by the Spanish, the state and skeptical archaeologists were not going to accept the identification of Mel's shipwreck as the *Atocha* until the main hull was found. It was the archaeological challenge of a lifetime, and I couldn't simply walk away from it. Mel had found his archaeologist.

Silver Bars

Above is a silver ingot taken from the wreck of Nuestra Señora de Atocha. The symbol at the left end of the bar (which measures over 12 inches) is the Shipper's Mark (note the same symbol on the page of the ship's manifest. The roman numerals (shown reversed) to the right of the center line reads 569, which is the ingot number.

The "bite" taken by the assayer to determine the fineness of the silver.

The talley number, 4,584.

The"D" may stand for Delvas, the Portuguese who held the slave contract in 1622.

The Ley states the fineness of the silver, 2,380 out of a possible 2,400. This is very fine silver.

This ingot, one of the first discovered on the Atocha, was sent by the Royal Treasury to King Philip IV for tax collected on black slaves sold in Cartagena.

The contemporary drawing of the Monte de Plata shows the concept of the fabulous wealth of the New World. It shows the interior of a "mountain of silver" mined by slave laborers at Potosi.

chapter 5

Identifying the Wreck

Having accepted the political and professional problems that the *Atocha* project would inevitably cause, I was anxious to tackle the archaeological challenge: using the artifacts to reconstruct the ship and find the main hull.

Before the anatomy of the wreck site could be explained, some major questions had to be clearly defined. The biggest question was the proper identification of the wreck. If we could confirm that it was a galleon, and that it was the *Atocha* we would have a good idea of the ship's general construction and a great deal of information about what artifacts we could expect to find.

There seemed to be two alternative theories, only one of which could be true. The first theory was that the site was the wreck of the *Nuestra Señora de Atocha*. But seven other ships also sank on September 6, 1622. It was possible that Treasure Salvors had found one of these. Theory two, therefore, was that the site was the wreck of another ship of the 1622 *flota*.

Two archaeological questions sprang from these theories. First, did the artifacts on the site indicate that the wreck was an early-17th century vessel and that it was part of the 1622 treasure fleet? Second, did the artifacts show that the site was in fact the *Atocha*? Of course, there were the silver ingots with markings that matched those listed on the *Atocha*'s manifest. However, some archaeologists supported Burt Webber's contention that these may not have come from the wreck of the *Atocha*, but could have been transferred from it to any other ship in the fleet. Also, the Spanish had tried to salvage the *Atocha*. Could this be a Spanish salvage vessel that had wrecked with some recovered *Atocha* treasure aboard?

With appropriate questions in hand, we were ready to let the artifacts speak for the wrecksite, to let them tell us what they could about the ship. One traditional way of dating an archaeological site is through the style and design of the artifacts.

The *Atocha* was a military vessel. A number of small arms had been brought up, and the types of weapons and their design could help give us an approximate date and confirm whether the wreck was that of a military or civilian ship. So far, the divers had brought up 34 muskets and arquebuses, 44 swords, and 15 daggers. While the weapons were heavily encrusted, all of the muskets and arquebuses appeared to have matchlock firing mechanisms of the type used by Western European armies throughout most of the 16th and 17th centuries. Although the wheellock firing mechanism was introduced between 1500 and 1550, matchlock was simpler and cost less to build and maintain. The expense of the wheellock delayed its acceptance, and it wasn't in common use until the late 1600s. The same was true of the flintlock, which was invented in the late 1500s but wasn't common until a century later.

The firearms were heavily encrusted with coral and iron concretions, making it impossible to compare them to firearms in museum collections whose date of manufacture was known. So while the muskets and arquebuses didn't give us a firm date, they also didn't suggest a date later than 1630.

Among the swords recovered, the design of the 30 rapiers offered the best chance for accurate dating. Swords of the medieval era (1000-1480 A.D.) were heavy, and were designed for slashing and cutting. A different style of swordplay, called fencing, spread through Europe during the Renaissance (1300-1500 A.D.). Fencing relied on thrusting and parrying rather than slashing and cutting, and as a result, a new kind of sword—the rapier—evolved. As fencing techniques developed, the rapier went through a series of design changes. Early on, some rapier blades were over five feet long and featured elaborate guard hilts to keep opponents' blades from piercing the swordsman's hand. Throughout the 16th century, blades gradually became shorter and guard hilts less elaborate. During this time, Spanish craftsmen developed the high-quality Toledo steel, and the Spanish cities of Toledo and Valencia became the leading centers of rapier making.

The swords recovered from the wrecksite were also heavily encrusted. The longest blades measured about three feet in length, indicating they'd been manufactured sometime after shorter blades became popular. X-rays were taken of 26 encrusted hilts, from which we were able to make two critical observations. First, some showed an S-shaped hilt—the type of swept-hilt rapier common throughout Western Europe from about 1570 to 1630. Second, there were no cup-hilt rapiers. Cup-shaped rapier hilts were especially popular in Spain and

This illustration of a musketeer holding a matchlock musket is circa 1607.

The matchlock was a firearm designed to fire when a slow burning match, or lighted taper was brought in contact with a priming powder. The matchlock mechanism was a simple design. The outside of the lock was a forked holder for the match or taper, called a serpentine. The sear, on the inside of the lock, connected the serpentine to the trigger. When the trigger was pressed, it brought the lit serpentine in contact with the priming powder. The flash ignited the charge in the barrel by a small hole (touch hole) drilled through the barrel breech.

This lead musket shot ranged in diameter from 5/8 to 7/8 inch. These little lead balls were found in great quantities at both the Margarita and Atocha wrecksites.

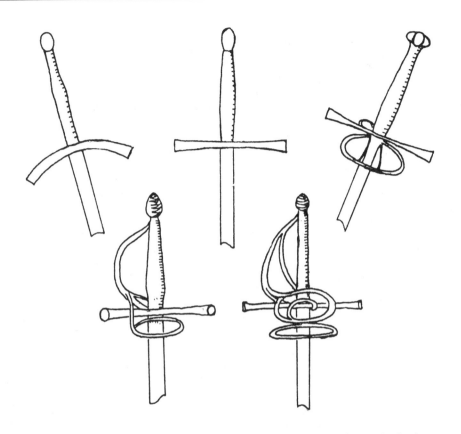

The first quarter of the 17th Century was a time of transition in rapier design. Slowly, the simpler early style of sword hilts gave away to even more elaborate designs. The five basic types of hilts found on the Atocha site included simple cross hilts or estocs and several variations of the swept hilt, popular in Europe from about 1570 to 1630.

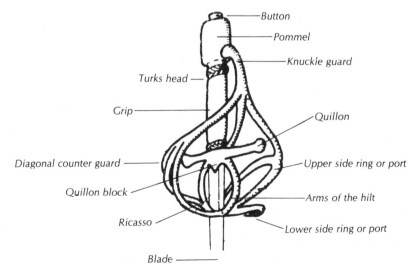

Italy during the second quarter of the 17th century. Both of these observations supported a date early in the 17th century.

Traditionally, archaeologists have relied on analysis of pottery to date sites. This works well for some land sites, where recognizable variations in the design and decoration of pottery occurred over relatively short periods of time.

Although there was a large assortment of glazed and unglazed pottery, little documentation exists dating types of Spanish colonial earthenware. Some of the most distinctive ceramics on the site were fragments of large vessels called olive jars. They are the most common pottery on shipwrecks of this period. Archaeologists had given them that name because initially they were believed to have been used to carry olives. Actually, they were used to carry a great many things, and were the five-gallon utility cans of the era. The olive jars were all of the type defined as "Middle Style," which has been dated by Hispanic scholars to the period 1580-1750.

Other ceramics from the site included three blue on white sherds of Chinese porcelain, which were too small for positive identification. Chinese porcelain was a luxury good from the Orient being shipped through America to Europe. It was shipped from the Philippines to Acapulco via the Manila fleet, then transported overland to Vera Cruz, where it was picked up by the New Spain fleet.

Three other sherds were recognized as Indian pottery. What were they doing on the wrecksite? Was Meso-American Indian ware being shipped back to Europe as curios, or were they used as kitchen wares by the Spaniards on the ship? The Spanish records showed that Calusa Indians living on the Marquesas Keys were involved in the early efforts to salvage the ship. Were these sherds proof of the salvage effort? The answers to these questions would have to wait.

Other ceramic pieces found included tin-glazed earthenware known as majolica, which is commonly found on Spanish colonial land sites. Archaeologists have dated majolica by type and design, and illustrations of these designs have been published. From the wreck there were three complete bowls of a style known as Colombia Plain (produced on land sites from 1493-1650); two sherds of Ichtucknee Blue on Blue (1550-1650); one sherd of Ichtucknee Blue on White (1615-1650); and one sherd of Santo Domingo Blue on White (1550-1630). By comparing the pottery found on the wrecksite to pottery from land sites, we saw that the wreck had yielded one style of majolica that wasn't produced before 1615, and another type that wasn't produced after about 1630. The ship, therefore, had to date between 1615 and 1630; *prima facie* archaeological evidence that this site was of a ship that had sunk in 1622.

Coins are another way to identify a shipwreck. Over the years, coin collectors—numismatists— and historians have accumulated a great deal of information on the design of the dies used to strike *reales* and *doubloons*, and the names of various mint masters and assayers. The coins recovered from the wreck that had been studied included coins struck during the reigns of three Spanish kings—Philip II, Philip III, and Philip IV. The coins listing Philip IV as sovereign couldn't have been minted prior to the first year of his reign, which was 1621. Alberto Pradeau, a numismatic historian whose *Numismatic History of Mexico* is one of the definitive works on Spanish colonial coinage, examined coins from the site and confirmed that none had been minted after 1622. The date was fixed. The coins told us that the wreck could not have gone down prior to 1621, and we had found no coins minted after 1622.

Still, it wasn't necessarily the *Atocha*. There was one other possibility that the site was that of a Spanish salvage vessel carrying coins recovered from the 1622 fleet. In 1625, a small vessel sent from Havana to maintain the buoys left by Vargas and Cardona over the wrecksite had disappeared. But the types of artifacts found led us to the inescapable conclusion that this site was a galleon. The pieces brought up were definitely those that would be expected on the major vessels of a treasure fleet. Gold and silver bullion, coins, infantry weapons, navigational instruments (including the marine astrolabe), gold chains and jewelry, stone cannon shot, and religious objects all argued that this was a galleon. A merchant ship would have carried few small arms; certainly not enough to outfit an entire company of foot soldiers. It's highly unlikely that the divers aboard a Spanish salvage ship would have wasted their time bringing up stone cannonballs or matchlock muskets that had been immersed in seawater for more than a year, ruling out the possibility that this was a lost salvage vessel. Also, indigo had been found mixed in with the other artifacts. A salvage ship wouldn't have been carrying indigo and the divers wouldn't have bothered to recover indigo from a galleon wreck.

Some rough sketches of the site showed that the pattern of artifacts on the bottom was definitely aligned on the axis of the anchor that had been found in 1971. That anchor, with a shaft over 15 feet long, was very similar in size to those previously recovered from other galleon wrecksites in Florida. Small salvage ships carried much smaller anchors. The divers had found large ballast stones, some almost 30 inches in diameter and weighing up to 100 pounds.

The wreck was unmistakably that of a galleon and one that sank in 1622. But which one? Three galleons went down in the storm: *Atocha*, *Margarita* and *Rosario*. Gaspar de Vargas salvaged the *Rosario* immediately after the hurricane. His salvage account placed the site of that ship in the Dry Tortugas, just off Loggerhead Key within the modern boundaries of Fort Jefferson National Monument. Our current position was far to the east of the Tortugas, so it had to be either the *Atocha* or the *Margarita*.

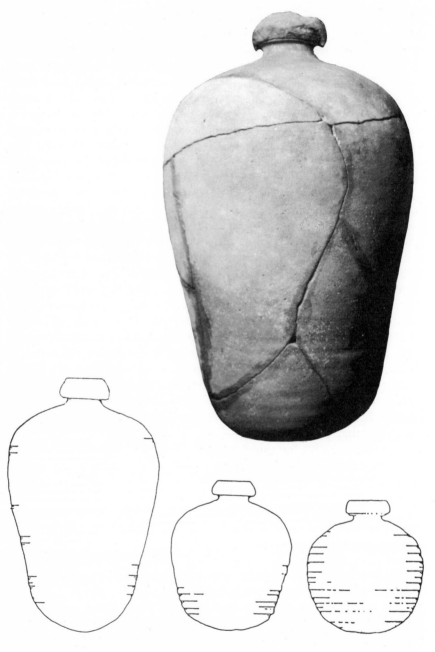

The small number of olive jars, similar to this one, found on the wrecksite was an indication that the main part of the ship was not in the Quicksands area surrounding the anchor. Olive jars were used to carry a wide variety of goods during a voyage, from wine to be traded in the Americas to agricultural products being returned to Spain and provisions for the passengers and crew. A large galleon may have carried as many as 1000 olive jars in her lower hull.

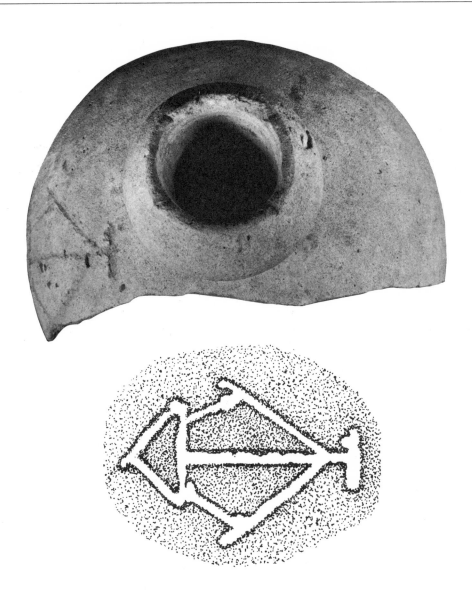

Some of the most distinctive ceramics on the site were fragments of olive jars. Archaeologists had given them that name because initially they were believed to have been used to carry olives. The olive jars were all of the type defined as "middle style", which has been dated by Hispanic scholars to the period 1580–1750. The design on this olive jar is probably a shipper's mark.

The Archive documents found by Gene Lyon listed the *Atocha* as having gone down 48 nautical miles east of the *Rosario*, about the distance from Loggerhead Key to this site. However, the documents also showed that the *Atocha* and *Margarita* sank close together. Captain de Lugo, who survived the sinking of the *Margarita*, said he had seen the *Atocha* sink one Spanish league (about three miles) east of the *Margarita*. Which site was it, the *Atocha* or *Margarita*? The three silver ingots, which displayed markings identical to those listed on the *Atocha*'s manifest, seemed to us to positively identify the site as that of the *Atocha*.

Others weren't convinced. Perhaps ingots were on other ships with serial numbers identical to those being shipped on the *Atocha*. Or, others postulated, the ingots could have been transferred from *Atocha* to *Margarita*, or to any other ship in the fleet before the sinking. We considered that highly unlikely. The record-keeping of the Spanish *escribanos* was almost fanatically precise. If such a transfer had been made, it would have been reflected in the manifest.

Gene Lyon knew the manifest and the records in the Archive better than any other researcher on earth. He was convinced this was the *Atocha*. And I was convinced he was right.

We had a dilemma. If this site was in fact the *Atocha*, two years of digging had failed to uncover a number of artifacts that could be expected on the wreck of a large galleon. Where were the cannons? The Archive documents showed that the *Atocha* had 20 bronze cannons on board when she went down. Also, we'd found very little iron rigging. Only one anchor had been located. Gene had found the construction specifications for the *Atocha*, which indicated that the ship carried five main anchors weighing about 2,200 pounds each plus a smaller stream anchor weighing 500 pounds. Had they all been lost during the storm in an attempt to anchor before the ship foundered in the shallows? Had the divers simply missed four huge anchors?

There were more unanswered questions. While there were well-preserved wooden musket stocks and some wooden pieces believed to have been used to keep the ship's cargo in position, there were no traces of the wooden hull. If this was the site of the disintegration of a 550-ton galleon, the lower part of the hull would almost certainly have been preserved under the deep sands of the Marquesas.

Only one small architectural piece from the ship's hull had been identified: rudder pintles which attached the rudder to the ship's stern. At the time Mel's exploratory contract with the state didn't allow the divers to bring up anything from the site without the specific agreement of the State Marine Archaeologist. Even though this was a crucial piece of archaeological evidence, the state instructed Mel to throw the rudder pintles back in the ocean along with musket balls, silver spoons, and coins to satisfy their contract regulations. Mel's divers knew they were throwing away priceless artifacts; the rudder pintles were particularly important as there were very few such ship's fittings preserved in a study collection anywhere in the country. Although attempts were made to relocate the pintles, they were never found.

Other details nagged at us. The number of olive jars recovered was meager compared to the number recovered from galleons of the 1715 and 1733 fleets. We could expect perhaps as many as 500 jars or more on the *Atocha*, but fewer than 50 had been found.

What's more, there was no ballast pile. A 550-ton galleon would have carried an enormous load of rocks in her lower hull to lower the center of gravity and help keep her upright in the water. Ballast piles marking the location of the main hulls of the 1715 and 1733 galleons were over 100 feet long, 35 feet wide, and about five feet high. The ballast pile of the *San Angustias*, a 1733 wreck which was about the same size as the *Atocha*, was 90 feet long, 30 feet wide, and three feet high. Where was the enormous mound of rocks the *Atocha* carried in her belly?

The site seemed to conflict with some of the Spanish documents, too. The topographical features of the area didn't correspond to the historical records left by Vargas. Vargas had located the *Atocha* shortly after she sank, and recorded the depth of the water at the site as "ten *brazas*," or 54 feet. The accounts of the later salvors, Melián and Cardona, also indicated that the wreck lay much deeper than the 25 feet of water that surrounded the site of the anchor. Even allowing for the build-up of sediment over the years, the limestone bedrock at the site was at most 40 feet from the surface.

Clearly, there were two contradictory streams of evidence. An analysis of the artifacts showed that we had a major galleon. The ceramics and particularly the coins showed that it was indeed part of the 1622 fleet. And the silver ingots confirmed that it was the *Atocha*. Yet, the main hull was still missing. We had found the scene of the murder and clearly identified the victim. Now, where was the corpse?

chapter 6

The Deep Water Theory

There were three possible explanations for the conflicting evidence on this wrecksite. First, perhaps Burt Webber and the others were right about the silver ingots having been transferred off the *Atocha*. Perhaps the site was not the *Atocha* but the *Margarita*. The lack of ballast and the depth of the water corresponded well to accounts of Melián's salvage of the *Atocha's* sister ship. That would also explain the lack of large numbers of coins and silver ingots.

Second, if this was the *Atocha*, perhaps our digging procedures weren't methodical enough. Maybe we'd missed major concentrations of artifacts that still lay buried in the deep sand near the anchor.

Third, it seemed possible that the area around the anchor was only a part of the *Atocha* rather than the complete ship. If the galleon had broken apart as it went down, then more artifacts—and the motherlode—could still be with the main part of the hull, possibly located in deeper water southeast of the anchor.

If theory one was correct, and this was the *Margarita*, a methodical sweep of the area around the anchor should turn up conclusive proof. According to salvage records, Melián and Cardona salvaged a great deal of material from the *Margarita*, but had never recovered some 150 silver ingots, a large quantity of coins, copper ingots, and twelve bronze cannons. We should be able to find these materials and perhaps salvage equipment, such as grapnel hooks and drag lines, that had been lost during the salvage effort.

More digging would also confirm or disprove theory two, that the divers had simply missed the major artifacts in their previous searches.

Gold Chains and Jewelry

The great number of gold chains recovered from these two shipwrecks has puzzled archaeologists and historians. Ranging in length from a few inches to an amazing 12 feet, and weighing as much as 6½ pounds, these chains were most likely the personal property of wealthy passengers. On the overleaf is a close-up of one of the finest gold chains recovered from the Margarita site. Each gold link was individually hand made.

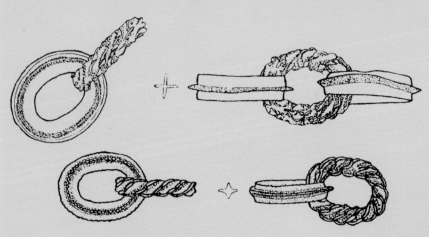

During the early part of the 17th century, Spain's dwindling wealth was highly concentrated in the Court and in the Church. In an effort to stabilize the economy, ostentatious displays of jewelry were discouraged. These articles were probably the possessions of wealthy merchants and travelers.

Some links appear to be of a precise weight related to the gold escudo coins of the period. Links of some of the chains are believed to have been used as a "money chain." Links could have been bent off and used in business transactions.

Bits of gold, gold coins, and links from some gold chains all had negotiable value.

This gold bosun's whistle worked perfectly when recovered. Found on the site of the Margarita, the whistle was used to communicate orders pertaining to shifting the sails to crewmen who might be far above the deck in the rigging.

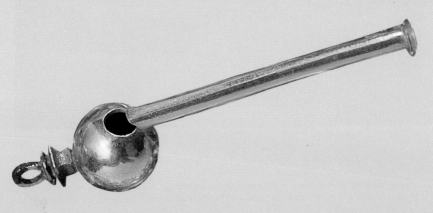

The mines of Colombia spewed forth a marvelous wealth of emeralds. Some were shipped to Spain uncut while others were cut, polished and set in mountings by native goldsmiths.

For years, Mel Fisher maintained that a large shipment of uncut emeralds was on board the Atocha even though no such shipment was listed on the ship's manifest. Many of the divers were skeptical of Mel's story until these uncut emeralds were found. More than 400 emeralds have been uncovered near the main ballast pile.

The lost-wax casting process used by Meso-American goldsmiths produced exquisite, finely detailed jewelry. The intricacy of the casting amazed Benvenuto Cellini, the master gold and silversmith of the Italian Renaissance.

These coins, more symmetrical than most are two-escudo's minted in Seville, Spain. They were probably the pocket change of the affluent passengers on board the Atocha.

The Belt

Boat captain John Brandon located the links of this gold belt on March 18, 1982 using the *Aqua Pulse III*, a prototype metal detector that can discriminate between ferrous and nonferrous metals. The style of the belt suggests to art historians that it was crafted in the 1500s, making it an heirloom long before the *Atocha* sank.

It took several months of careful cleaning and research by Jim Sinclair to determine that these exquisite gold links were actually part of a jewel encrusted belt. Each individual link is set with a single gem—rubies, pearls, and diamonds. Archaeologists presume that each gem came from a different part of the world: rubies from southeast Asia; pearls from the Island of Margarita off the Venezuelan coast; and the diamonds from northern South America.

Because pearls are organic, those mounted in the belt disintegrated long before it was recovered. For exhibition purposes, some were replaced by modern pearls.

This portrait of Philip II's daughter, showing her wearing similar gold links in her necklace and belt has helped to date the gold links found on the Atocha site. The many exquisite jewelry items recovered from Spanish shipwrecks pre-dating 1750 provide new information about the gradual transition of art styles from the Renaissance to the Baroque period. The designs, materials, and techniques used by artists and craftsmen during the 16th and 17th centuries not only reflect the final vestiges of Medieval art, but also the humanistic and classical ideas of the Renaissance which played a dominant role in shaping Western thought.

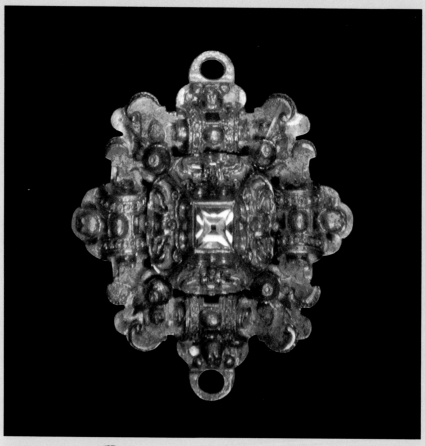

This detail of a single link from the belt reveals exquisite craftsmanship. Dr. Priscilla E. Muller, museum curator of the Hispanic Society of America, has been studying this heirloom to ascertain its origin. While it's likely that the belt was made in Europe, the styling reflects the influence of Meso-American Indian goldsmiths.

The digging, however, had to be carefully orchestrated. Precise site maps were the only way to plot the spatial relationship of the artifacts and begin to piece together the sequence of the sinking. The methods that had been adopted by treasure hunters in the 1960s were simply not precise enough to solve the mystery of the *Atocha* and find the motherlode. We needed to create a clearly delineated search grid on the surface of the water covering this vast site and then reproduce that grid on the ocean floor. We needed new techniques for mapping the sea bed and recording the location of artifacts, not only in terms of their distance from two edges of the grid, but also showing the amount of sand that covered them. Our map of the site had to be truly three dimensional, like a geologist's map that shows features both above and below ground level.

For me, the big question was this: To what extent could the treasure divers be taught the importance of archaeological record keeping, and how could they be inspired to exercise the patience to do it correctly, over and over again? These divers were not archaeology students already trained in the basic techniques of site mapping, they were young adventurers. They'd signed up with Mel to bring silver and gold up from the bottom, not to produce endless reams of paperwork. This was the crux of the argument that my archaeologist colleagues used to discredit any excavation conducted by commercial salvage divers.

I knew the divers weren't about to help me map the site unless they understood clearly how it was going to help find the motherlode. This meant slowly teaching the most interested divers about artifacts and how they could be used to establish a trail back to the main treasure pile. Some of them already knew quite a bit about coins, and some had studied other types of artifacts as well. My job was to show the divers that we needed one another. I needed their underwater experience and knowledge of the site, and they needed my ability to analyze archaeological records. Working together, I was sure we could find the motherlode.

I had become an apostle of archaeology among a bunch of treasure hunters. Could it work? Or were my critics right—was I deluding myself? The purists in the shipwreck community were already openly derisive and were doing everything they could to undercut my efforts. My hopes, whatever their validity, were founded in my previous land experience.

During the time I had worked in Jamaica and Ghana, I trained university students in field archaeology and taught unskilled laborers scientific digging techniques. In Ghana, I excavated archaeological sites with African tribesmen for six years. I didn't speak their language, and they didn't speak English, so all of my instructions were relayed by an interpreter. I felt that, if I could teach Ghanians without speaking their native language, surely I could teach Mel's divers. There was a "language" difficulty, here, too. Because I had spent so much time out of the United States, I had missed the significant events that had shaped their lives and their perceptions: Kennedy's assassination, the civil rights movement, the Vietnam War, rock 'n' roll music, the counterculture movement, drugs, and Woodstock. I had very little in common with them; I was, once more, an outsider. How could I just appear on their wrecksite and begin telling them they were doing things "wrong?"

I did know one thing. If I could succeed in working with these eager young divers, I could demonstrate to the government archaeologists in Tallahassee and Washington that there was a better way to deal with treasure hunters. The intent of their adversarial policy was to place shipwrecks off limits to anyone without university credentials. This meant that a good deal of knowledge about America's maritime origins might never be recovered. What if treasure hunters could be trained to help archaeologists, and shown that good archaeology enhanced their profits? Paraprofessionals are used in other highly specialized fields—law and medicine, for instance. Not everything has to be done by a surgeon. Trained paramedics are perfectly capable of giving first-aid and stabilizing a patient while waiting for a physician to operate. Why couldn't treasure hunters help me to rescue information?

Finding the motherlode of the *Atocha* was the Mt. Everest of New World shipwrecks. If that could be done with a degree of archaeological propriety while using salvage divers, it could be done on other New World wrecks as well.

Mapping the artifacts on the *Atocha* site was an arduous task. Slowly, Mel's divers began to get excited about learning archaeological techniques. From memory, they helped reconstruct the locations of finds made prior to 1973. One night aboard the *Virgilona*, two of them, John Brandon and Spencer Wickens, came to me with a crude site map they had pieced together. The major finds of the past three years were clearly marked. The map had no scale and wasn't much to look at, but it was a place to start. A lot of effort went into that crude map, which they'd sketched on the back of a paper plate. As we studied it, we realized that, somewhere underneath the catsup stains and the grease, were clues. Recognized and properly read, they could lead us to the motherlode. The crew was ready to start mapping the site precisely.

The wrecksite was about nine miles west of the Marquesas. The shallow water surrounding the anchor gradually deepened to the southeast, leading out to Hawk Channel—which passes close on the inside of the Outer Reef. Beyond the Outer Reef is the Florida Straits and the main shipping channel lying between Key West and Cuba.

The anchor had been found in about 25 feet of water on the southern edge of an area known as the "Quicksands." The name didn't mean the area swallowed divers, but that the bottom was covered with a sand composed of loose shell fragments that are constantly shifted by the waves and tides. The result is a series of sinuous "dune" formations on the bottom. Tidal channels cross these dunes, running from northeast to southwest. Around the anchor, the sand is nearly 15 feet deep. Below it is a bed of limestone, the surface of which is rippled and pocked with small hollows and crevices. The sand piled on top of the limestone gradually thins out until it disappears about a quarter of a mile from the anchor. Southeast of the Quicksands, the water depth increases gradually to about 40 feet, and the sand covering the bedrock thins out to a veneer just two and a half inches thick. Small sponges and sea fans grow in this area, which we called the Coral Plateau. Continuing to the southeast, away from the anchor, the Coral Plateau slopes downward into the "Mud Deep." Here, the bedrock dips sharply, possibly following the channel of a river that may have flowed through the area when it was above sea level thousands of years ago. This channel is filled with muddy silt. On the other side of the Mud Deep is an area populated by scattered colonies of star coral and brain coral called the Patch Reef. Immediately south of the Patch Reef is Hawk Channel. On the other side of Hawk Channel lies a much larger, continuous reef line known as the Outer Reef, and finally, the edge of the Continental Shelf. The Continental Shelf is where the North American continent drops off into the deep ocean separating Cuba from the Florida Peninsula.

We couldn't cover so vast an area with a reliable and practical mapping grid, so we first concentrated on the area surrounding the anchor. We laid out cables marking off a "corridor" aligned southeast to northwest on both sides of the ·galleon anchor, which we called the galleon anchor corridor. Resembling a tic-tac-toe board inside a square, the lines stretched about 400 yards, from the anchor to just beyond the edge of the Quicksands. This area was subdivided into four sections by lines crossing the site side to side. The locations of these lines were marked by eight surface buoys. Under water, buoys were placed along the grid lines every 50 feet. Thus horizontal reference points were established both on the water surface and the ocean floor.

As the salvage boats used their mailboxes to dig holes from above, the position of each hole was mapped by taking measurements off the surface buoys. Additional measurements were then also taken. Using a Brunton compass mounted on a table, we took three bearings from mid-ship and compared them to bearings taken from the stern, to mark the boat's position within a range of about ten feet. This was half of the diameter of most of the holes dug in the Quicksands. We could get even higher accuracy by taking the bearings with a sextant instead of the Brunton compass. Using our grid and these bearings, we checked that the holes were dug close enough together to locate whatever artifacts might be in the galleon anchor corridor.

As the digging began, all of the holes were numbered. The artifacts recovered from the various holes were listed on a standardized data form. Artifact maps were drawn from the information on these forms. From the maps, it soon became clear that the upper layer of sand on the site was being moved by the tidal current while the lower level of sand seemed to be relatively stable. Therefore, instead of one artifact scatter pattern, we had two.

The heavier objects, such as ballast stones, ingots, and clumps of coins, had moved down through the shifting sand into the lower, stationary layer. The lighter artifacts, such as potsherds, barrel hoops, and individual coins, were found in the upper layer of sand. This layer was constantly shifting, moving the clusters of artifacts with it. As a result, the pattern of artifacts in the upper layer was displaced slightly off the central axis of the pattern of heavy material in the lower layer. This pattern of heavy material was the real "footprint" of the wreck that we would need to trace to find the motherlode. Its true outlines had been blurred by the shifting of the lighter artifacts in the drifting sands above, but we could never have known that if we hadn't mapped the site. I kept thinking back to Carl Clausen's 1965 statement, based on the 1715 wreck, that there was no real pattern to the artifacts of a shallow water shipwreck. Now I knew he had been wrong.

As the pattern developed on our site map, we realized that, ironically, it was the rocks that could tell the most about the location of the treasure. The pattern of the heavy ballast, which had moved little over the years, seemed the best way to pinpoint where the ship had hit the shallow water on the edge of the Quicksands. Maps of the ballast deposits soon showed that the largest concentration lay just within the edge of the Quicksands in about a yard of sand. This was the center of what the divers called "The Bank of Spain," the area where the three silver ingots, 4,000 coins, the astrolabe, and gold jewelry were found. Clearly, this was where the ship had hit the Quicksands. From this point, the ballast scatter spread to the northwest. A series of overlapping holes dug by the *Virgilona* and *Southwind* across the scatter pattern showed that the ballast was laid out in a strip about 50 feet wide. Its axis was aligned on the site of the galleon anchor. This clearly delineated strip ruled out the theory that the *Atocha* might have rolled to one side or the other as it broke up in the shallows. If the main part of the wreck was in the Quicksands, it had to be inside the galleon anchor corridor. From the edge of the Quicksands to the galleon anchor, the ballast quickly thinned. Ballast concentrations were heaviest around the Bank of Spain and lightest at the other end of the corridor, around the anchor.

The amount of ballast was a concern as well. Some ballast had been found and moved prior to 1973, and there was no record of how much. Relying on the memory of divers who were present at that time and records of the amount uncovered in the present digging, we estimated that about 70 to 80 tons of ballast had been found in the galleon anchor corridor. A complete galleon with a 550-ton displacement should have carried twice that amount.

While we had failed to find the *Atocha's* motherlode, the digging during 1973 and 1974 was a success. The systematic search had convinced us that there was no bulk of cargo, cannons, anchors, or remnants of a hull in the immediate Quicksands area.

We had started our digging with three alternative theories: One, that this was the site of the *Margarita* instead of the *Atocha*; two, that the *Atocha's* main hull was within the galleon anchor corridor; and three, that the main hull was elsewhere. Two of those possibilities had been eliminated.

It was now clear that this was *not* the site of the *Margarita*. There just wasn't enough ballast or cargo in the area. Also, the lack of artifacts showed us that the main part of the *Atocha* was not here either. That left our third theory: The main part of the *Atocha* was elsewhere.

So far, our search efforts had been concentrated northwest and southeast of the Bank of Spain, and with good reason. The Quicksands area had thus far produced the greatest concentration of gold and silver. The artifacts found to date, and the amount and pattern of the ballast, showed that the galleon anchor corridor contained material from the break up of a part of the ship, probably her sterncastle. The astrolabe was probably the personal property of the chief pilot and would have been kept in his cabin in the sterncastle. The gold coins were the pocket change of wealthy passengers, also quartered in the stern. Our map of the artifact scatter showed a distinct trail that led from the Quicksands area, which was located in approximately 25 feet of water, southeastward toward deeper water—about 40 feet. Vargas had noted in his salvage account that the *Atocha* sank in 55 feet of water.

We also knew that the ship was intact when Vargas and Lopez first spotted it, the mizzenmast sticking up above the water. It seemed likely that the top decks of the *Atocha* had been torn away by the second hurricane, the one that had hit on October 5 while Vargas was salvaging the *Rosario* at Loggerhead Key. No wonder the mizzenmast had disappeared when Vargas returned to search for the *Atocha*.

Based on this information, and the alignment of shipwreck material in the galleon anchor corridor, we suspected that the motherlode was between the edge of the Quicksands and the Patch Reef to the southeast, an area which we called the Southeast Corridor. Apparently, the detached superstructure had been swept from deep water into the shallows, and hit the edge of the Quicksands in the area of the Bank of Spain. The lower hull, beneath the turn of the bilge, should be relatively intact. Inside were the 500 olive jars we hadn't found, the 80 or so tons of ballast that was missing, and, of course, the motherlode—Mel Fisher's $400 million treasure.

chapter 7

History in Bronze

Our search was now concentrated in deeper water. As the *Virgilona* criss-crossed the Patch Reef, its magnetometer registered small concentrations of metal objects. The Navy had used the Quicksands area as a bombing range, littering the site with bomb fragments and other refuse. We found plenty of metal, but not the main ballast pile. Don Kincaid and Pat Clyne, both experienced divers and photographers, helped me organize a thorough magnetometer survey of the Patch Reef and the Southeast Corridor. Unfortunately, this survey didn't pick up any substantial signs of shipwreck debris. Did this mean that there was no wreckage trail in this direction, or had we failed to locate any artifacts?

I was almost convinced that the *Atocha*'s hull lay in deeper water along the line of wreck scatter. The first confirmation of this theory came in the fall of 1974 when we found a fist-sized ballast stone and an iron object that resembled a flattened wrought iron bowl less than a quarter mile from the inner edge of the Patch Reef. Most of the divers believed that the iron object was a bomb fragment, but there was no question about the origin of this ballast rock. It was the same type of rock we had found scattered throughout the Quicksands area.

We were elated with our find, but puzzled at not having discovered more remains of the *Atocha* in the Southeast Corridor. I wondered whether the galleon had come in from the southeast, struck the Patch Reef and then sunk between the reef and the Quicksands. We renewed the search for artifacts leading out from the Bank of Spain toward Hawk Channel. If we could find the scattered shipwreck and follow its trail, we should eventually come across the *Atocha*'s rich cargo.

In January 1975, Gene Lyon and I began an intensive study of the artifacts that had been recovered in an attempt to understand their relationship to the site and the historical accounts of the shipwreck. Every bit of data that helped reconstruct the *Atocha*'s final hours might bring us closer to unraveling the great mystery. Ray McAllister, a professor of ocean engineering at Florida Atlantic University, examined a hydrographic model of the area. John Cryer, a former U.S. Navy meteorologist, helped put together a meteorological model of the 1622 hurricane. Working with an account of the *Margarita*'s journey, Cryer reconstructed the course of the fleet during the storm and determined the speed, direction, and course of the ships. Although he had no idea where we had found the wreck, his estimates placed the position of the two ships within a mile or so of our search area.

Meanwhile, in Seville, Gene prepared a lengthy analysis comparing our artifact inventory to the *Atocha*'s manifest. Among the thousands of historical documents, he uncovered a list of the *Atocha*'s bronze cannons, and a copy of the ship's construction contract, which provided new insight into the dimensions of the hull and rigging plan.

Though Gene and I firmly believed that the lower hull structure lay somewhere between the Mud Deep and Hawk Channel, other members of the Treasure Salvors crew were convinced that the galleon's riches lay in the Quicksands.

As spring brought warm winds and calm seas to the Marquesas, the crews renewed their exploration of the Quicksands area, particularly the stretch between the Bank of Spain and the galleon anchor. In March, diver Joe Spangler recovered a unique treasure: a gold whistle, earwax spoon, and manicure set. The gold bosun's whistle attached to a double length of gold neck chain, was most likely the property of a wealthy passenger.

Shortly after the *Southwind* and *Virgilona* moved to a new site northwest of the anchor divers pulled up two gold bars similar to the ones found in 1971. They had Roman numeral karat markings and weights marked in small Arabic numbers. And though the bars had been assayed, they carried no royal seals or mint marks. Were they contraband, being smuggled back to Spain? If not, could they be identified on the manifest?

In June 1975, Dirk Fisher returned from the commercial diving school he'd been attending with a new enthusiasm for my deep-water theory. He'd learned deep diving techniques, perhaps one of the reasons he became so excited about my theory. Within a month, he moved the refitted *Northwind* to the Mud Deep, where the crew would have to deal with a new bottom condition, hard-packed clay, limestone, and bedrock.

The *Northwind* was useful in this area because the wash from the tug's huge props was deflected straight down by mailboxes set at a

90-degree angle. Its sister ship, the *Southwind*, had mailboxes bent at a 45-degree angle rather than straight down. While this angle made the *Southwind* ideal for digging long, narrow trenches in the loose bottom of the Quicksands, out in deeper water, not enough power from the props reached the bottom to remove the hard-packed clay. Also, the angle of the tubes pushed the boat forward, causing her to drag anchor and making it difficult to precisely control the area being dug.

We hadn't yet gotten enough geological data on the Mud Deep to determine whether the hull would be visible on the sea floor or whether it would be completely buried in the silt. But new archaeological data from other wrecksites gave us some information to work with.

Don Kincaid and I surveyed the wreck of another of the 1622 ships, the small *patache*, or scout vessel, that had also sunk.

The *patache* had grounded in the Dry Tortugas. Bob Moran flew us over in his seaplane, giving us a good idea of what a virgin ballast pile from a 1622 wreck looked like. Although the *patache* was less than half the size of the *Atocha*, it had left a clearly visible ballast pile about 60 feet long and 20 feet wide. In less than ten feet of water we found pottery sherds, the ship's wooden rigs, and a well-preserved hull structure sticking out from below a mound of rocks three feet high.

This wreck proved to us that lower hulls and ballast piles can remain intact and be clearly visible from the surface in shallow water. Of course, the *Atocha's* hull could have been covered over with sand; but of the 21 wrecksites believed to be part of the 1733 Spanish *flota* which sank in the portion of Hawk Channel that extends north into the Middle Keys, very few of the ships were completely blanketed with silt and sand. Most of these wrecks were clearly visible on the bottom. In fact, the ballast pile of one of them, the *Herrera*, had been spotted from the air. It rested in the center of a sand pocket surrounded by grass in about 20 feet of water, along the inner edge of Hawk Channel.

Whether or not a ship's ballast pile is eventually covered by sand depends on how the ship sank and a number of environmental variables that we still don't understand thoroughly. The lower hull structures of the 1715 galleons, which sank in just 15 feet of water, were completely covered by sand when Mel and the Real 8 crews found them in the 1960s. Other ship structures as deep as 35 feet have been found fully exposed. It depends to a large extent on what archaeologists refer to as the "depositional environment" of the area. In a high-energy coastal region, with waves and storms constantly lashing the bottom, strong water currents create an underwater sand storm, eventually covering stationary objects with layers of sediment. In a low-energy area, such as a relatively deep offshore channel, water circulates more slowly and stirs up less sediment.

Knowing whether the hull would be exposed on the bottom would make our search easier. Given the nature of the bottom in Hawk

Channel, there seemed to be three possibilities: first, the heavy lower hull structure might have sunk through the sand and mud to bedrock. If this were the case, it was probably completely covered over by silt. Second, it may have sunk a short way into the mud leaving the portion of the hull projecting above the bottom partially covered by sediment. And of course, it was possible that the spill of ballast and cargo had lightened the hull, so that it was resting exposed on the bottom covered only by a light dusting of sand.

If the hull rested on bedrock under the sand, it would be impossible to locate from aerial photographs. Yet we knew from exploratory digging and sub-bottom sonar surveys that indicated the presence of objects beneath the sea bed that the bottom of Hawk Channel was primarily hard-packed clay with a thin veneer of sand and large coral heads rising up some eight to ten feet high. Though we didn't know the depth of the hard-packed clay that was sandwiched between the sand and bedrock, it seemed likely that this "hard pan" would resemble the surface area north of the Patch Reef. If so, this dense material, which lay three feet from the top of the sea bed, would have prevented the *Atocha's* hull structure from sinking to the bedrock. The hull would thus be partially visible on the bottom, unless it were covered by coral. A number of wrecks in the Caribbean have been found with as much as twelve feet of coral grown over them. But researchers have found that coral growth within the Florida Outer Reef tract is much slower than in the southern Caribbean, so this seemed unlikely.

So, our search of Hawk Channel and surveys of the *patache* had helped develop some useful working theories, but we still didn't have the motherlode. Treasure Salvor's staff was impatient. A chart of the wrecksite over Mel's desk told the whole story. Amid the marks denoting buoys, chains, and grids was a heavy mask of lines and circles detailing our mag runs, sonar surveys, and digs of the past four years. Within the company, we disagreed on the location of the main cargo. Mel challenged all of us to back up our theories with cash. Drawing a heavy circle on the chart he said, "Put up or shut up. That's where I think we'll find it. Bleth, Gene, Duncan—and the rest of you—put your money on the line and your mark on the map. Let's bet a week's pay and see who wins." I put my mark in the middle of Hawk Channel, in a small area of deep water directly in line with the Quicksands anchor.

Out at the site, the crews continued to dig the deeper water of the Southeast Corridor, straining to find a trace of the ballast trail. Then, early on Sunday, July 13, 1975, Dirk Fisher swam away from the *Northwind* to reset her anchors, which had dragged during the night. Dirk came up screaming. His wife, Angel, thought he had been attacked by a shark and panicked. But slowly, the crew crowding the railing of the search ship understood that Dirk was in no danger: he'd just found five of the *Atocha's* cannons lying fully exposed in 39 feet of water.

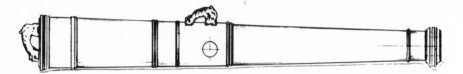

One of Bill Muir's archaeological drawings illustrates a bronze cannon believed to have been mounted on the stern of the Margarita, which was found in 1980. The cannon shows the same "leaping dolphin" style lifting rings as the bronze cannon found on the Atocha site in 1975. This cannon, however, is not nearly as well-preserved and its surface is heavily pitted by corrosion.

The cannons were used to fire a variety of projectiles, the most common of which were solid cannon balls made of iron, lead, or stone used to puncture an enemy's hull. This is a well-preserved cluster of grape shot—a sack of iron balls designed to scatter when fired. Grape shot turned the cannon into a giant shotgun, and was used at close range to rake an opponent's deck, disabling and killing the crew.

This gunnery scale provided the different measures of gunpowder needed for the various sizes of cannons and kinds of shot used aboard a galleon.

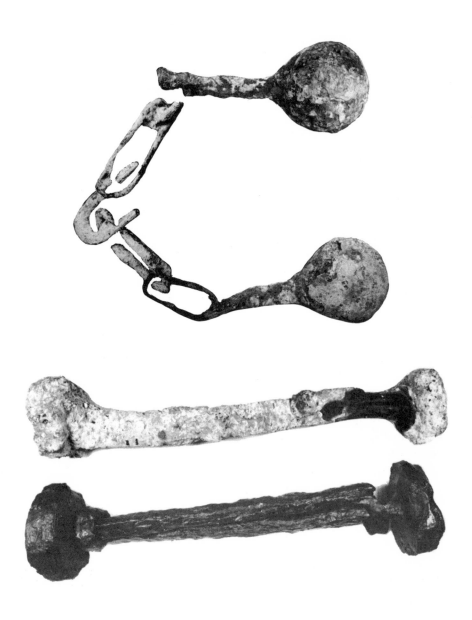

Chain shot and bar shot were fired into an opponent's rigging, shredding rigging lines, yardarms, and sails as they whirled through the air.

Once again, fate had intervened in our search. Dirk didn't dare move; he tread water over the cannons until the boat could be moved over the site. Don Kincaid and I immediately rushed out from the Key West office to map the area with a grid. Dirk agreed to shut down the whole operation so that we could lay a baseline for mapping the cannons and compile a photomosaic. The *Northwind* dug a pattern around the cannons, blowing loose sand off the sea bed.

As they began the fourth hole, Pat Clyne spied four more cannons. On both sides, the divers carefully moved the sand away from the cannons and photographed their positions so that I could determine the spatial relationship between the two groups. I stressed to the divers that the cannons didn't just fall randomly from the ship. The position of the cannons on the sea bed would tell us how and where they were placed on deck. More importantly, the relationship of the two cannon features would tell us the direction the sterncastle was headed before it grounded at the Bank of Spain. Following that line out to deep water should direct us to the hull.

The lay of the cannons raised more questions: Did the ship roll from one side to the other during the storm, hence dropping cannons off each side? Or did the cannons, which were located on either side of the ship, simply slide down the length of the deck and tumble off one end? Our research didn't answer either of these questions. But we knew that the part of the ship holding these cannons was the same part of the vessel which hit the Quicksands and broke up, spreading shipwreck materials toward the northwest.

The first group of cannons looked as if they'd fallen from the deck one after another. We could almost visualize strong gusts of wind heeling the galleon over to the left with such force that the first group of heavy cannons rolled off the gun deck. As the ship rocked back to the right, more cannons rolled off the deck, one after another as the floating ship's structure pitched from side to side. Finally, all nine cannons lay scattered on the sea bed. In the first cluster, the cannons rested in a random fashion. The first two lay almost crisscrossed, one on top of the other. The next two pointed directly west, while the last cannon pointed northwest.

The first group of cannons, which lay exposed on top of bedrock, were badly worn. The foundry marks, embellishments, and other engravings had eroded badly in the salt water. Time had removed character from the cannons. But the history and culture of 17th century Spain was written plainly on the barrels of the second group. Mel had been looking for bronze cannons all his life, but never found one. Now, the *Northwind* had found nine in one day. Mel came out to the site with champagne for a mid-afternoon celebration. After we mapped and photographed the cannons, we brought up the first two. In the midst of the partying, Angel helped clean off the encrustation so we could see the weight marking, which was inscribed near the breech moldings.

I savored the craftsmanship evident in the images of dolphins sculpted on the butt of the cannon. There was also a four-quartered shield—the coat of arms of the Spanish kings—and, below the touch-hole, the numbers "31 q 10L," the cannon's weight. During his last trip to Seville, Gene had found a list of the *Atocha's* bronze cannons complete with numbers, indicating their weights, which should be stamped on each barrel. He had encouraged us to locate the cannons, for these would be further proof that we had found the *Atocha*.

I ran to my briefcase for the list. Scanning the document, my eyes rested on the numbers 3110—a match! "Here it is," I shouted. "This cannon came from the *Atocha*." Though we hadn't located the primary deposit, the cannons were a link connecting the scattered remains found in the shallow Quicksands and the main part of the *Atocha*, which I believed was in deeper water.

We were ecstatic. After so many years of uncertainty, we felt sure that we would soon be living Mel's famous catch phrase, "Today's the Day." The cannons were a timely talisman. Coming as it had when everyone was discouraged and at odds over where to search, the discovery brought the team back together and rekindled our passion to find the lost galleon. A visit from a *National Geographic* film crew later that week further fueled our enthusiasm. And we had another reason to celebrate: It was Angel Fisher's birthday. She and Dirk planned a small celebration that night aboard the *Northwind*.

To these young people anchored in the still water of the Marquesas, miles from the nearest shore, this was indeed the life they had all dreamed of: good friends, good diving, the treasure of the motherlode seemingly close at hand. But before dawn the next day, their perfect world turned upside down when the *Northwind* capsized.

Don Kincaid and six other crew members were thrown into the water. As the survivors climbed onto the overturned hull, they realized that Donny Jonas, Jim Solanick, Rick Gage, Dirk and Angel Fisher were missing. But, suddenly, Jim Solanick squeezed through a porthole and surfaced. Donny Jonas, trapped in an air pocket in the engine room, found a flashlight floating near him. He grabbed the flashlight, took a deep breath and swam to safety.

But for Rick Gage and Angel and Dirk Fisher, there was no escape. The dream had ended. These three paid a high price for Dirk's discovery and his commitment to the deep water theory.

The tragic news struck the Key West office like a thunderbolt. It was hard for everyone to believe that something this terrible could happen just as our luck was improving. Moe Molinar and his crew on the *Virgilona* recovered the bodies while the rest of us tried to guess what had gone wrong. There seemed to be several factors going against the *Northwind*: it had a leaky bulkhead fitting that allowed some water into the bilge, and a malfunctioning valve and fuel shifting from one side of the boat to the other might have destabilized the vessel. Since everyone was sleeping, they were unaware of the problem until it was too late.

The loss of lives was not new to the company. Two years earlier Nikki Littlehales, 12-year-old son of *National Geographic* photographer, Bates Littlehales, had been sucked into the blowers and died of multiple wounds. Now we had three more deaths to deal with. Was it all worth it? Were we all paying a high price to pursue what seemed to be an impossible dream? For the first time, the loss of these three fine young people made me seriously question my role in the operation.

Mel chartered an airplane to fly the entire company to Vero Beach where Dirk and Angel were buried by the same minister who had married them just two years before. John Brandon, Spencer Wickens, Tim March, John "BJ" Lewis, Hugh Spinney, Pat Clyne, and Tom Ford were among the friends present to bid their last farewells.

In my two years with the company I had grown close to Dirk and Angel. They always shared my aspirations of conducting a thorough archaeological study on the site. Aside from Gene Lyon, Dirk had been the strongest supporter of the deep water theory. Angel took charge of the digging records on the *Northwind*. Whenever she had time, she sketched the artifacts as they were recovered. Together, they had become a vital part of our archaeological team.

A tragedy as regrettable as this can sometimes divide a company. But the deaths of Dirk, Angel, and Rick seemed to bring all of us closer together. The loss of human lives made my commitment to the *Atocha* all the more important. I couldn't abandon it now.

I became obsessed with my professional responsibilities on the site. Mel was driven by the lure of gold and silver; I was driven by the desire to do good archaeology. Whether my professional colleagues approved of it or not, Mel's obsession and my commitments were now irrevocably locked together. I no longer cared what my academic colleagues and the government bureaucrats thought. I was committed to the end, whatever that might bring.

A few days after the funeral the *Virgilona* was back on the site. Mel insisted that no attempt be made to raise the *Northwind*. It was later sold where it lay. Her sister ship, the *Southwind*, never returned to the site and was sold soon afterward. The *Southwind*'s captain, Kim Fisher, married and enrolled in college to pursue his education.

Not everyone rallied around the Fishers in their time of despair. State and federal officials conspired once again to regain jurisdiction over the site—a battle they had lost just a few months before. A new battle was brewing, one that would be fought in court for the next Seven years by Treasure Salvors' legal counsel, David Paul Horan.

My decision to pursue the trail to the motherlode affected my life well beyond my professional obligations. I had been working as a professional archaeologist for more than 15 years, but had received only a Bachelor of Arts degree in geology with a minor in anthropology from Dartmouth College. Several months after the sinking of the *Northwind,* I enrolled in a graduate program at Florida Atlantic University's Anthropology Department. I lived in Miami and commuted 120 miles to Key West to oversee the work on the site. Now I had to drive another 50 miles to Boca Raton three nights a week to complete my credits. It was a terrible strain on both me and my wife, Marie.

Going back to school at the age of 37 was painful, and many times I was tempted to quit. My supervisor, Dr. William H. Sears, gave me a lot of support. He had been involved with the state's shipwreck salvage programs while at the Florida State Museum in the early 1960s. He had been present at the meetings when Mel pleaded with the state to provide more archaeological assistance on the 1715 sites. Mel never got that help. It was Dr. Sears who encouraged me to use my archaeological work on the *Atocha* as the thesis for my Master's in Anthropology.

In concentrating on my thesis, I had pulled away from my work on the *Atocha* site. This gave me a clearer picture of what we did and didn't know about the site and what we had to do to find the motherlode. But this fresh outlook also showed me that until Treasure Salvors made a commitment to search Hawk Channel, very little new archaeological information would be found to lead us to the treasure. Finding gold and silver up in the Quicksands was satisfying—and profitable—but it just wasn't furthering our overall objectives. Salvage boats could find treasure for the next decade up beyond the Bank of Spain and still not get any closer to the main deposit. No matter what anyone in the company believed, I knew the treasure just wasn't there. The artifacts were speaking to me loud and clear. They all told me to go to the deep water in the middle of Hawk Channel. Until Mel heard the same message, there was very little I could do to help him.

chapter 8

Exploring
Hawk Channel

The deaths of Dirk and Angel Fisher and Rick Gage brought an end to the 1975 diving season. But we couldn't let that end our search for the *Atocha*. We all knew that our missing comrades would want us to stay with the hunt, wherever it might lead, until we'd found the treasure that had cost them their lives.

As fair weather returned to the Marquesas in the spring of 1976, we tried to pick up the trail where we had left off—with Dirk's bronze cannons. But the deeper water and different ocean floor in our new search area created a need for new ways to explore. Up to now, we had relied on the magnetometers and mailboxes, which worked well in loose sand. Once the magnetometers identified a promising area, the crew quickly dug survey holes with the mailboxes. Divers working around the holes could easily fan the fine sand to locate small artifacts in the sides of the craters.

Now we were working the area southeast of the cannons along the main axis that extended from the galleon anchor corridor through the cannons to Hawk Channel. We concentrated our search efforts in the Mud Deep. Unable to quickly punch holes through the dense hard pan to the bedrock, the search slowed to a crawl. The crews tried using small airlifts and water hoses hung off the side of a new boat, the *Arbutus*, to puncture the hard pan, but it was still slow going.

Mel was up to the challenge. If he lacked a boat with the big engines and props needed to blast down through the deeper water and clear out the hardpan, why not build a huge portable mailbox? If a big enough motor and prop could be mounted in a cylinder, it could be lowered right down to the bottom. Mel found a company willing to

Religious Artifacts

The importance of religion to the 17th-century Spaniard cannot be overestimated. Catholicism permeated every aspect of Spanish culture, and all of the mortal perils faced by Spanish seafarers were insignificant when compared to the immortal peril of dying in a state of sin. For this reason, most ships had at least one priest on board, and religious ceremonies were strictly observed at sea.

This silver jewel box looking much like a sardine can would normally have been opened at the lab at Treasure Salvors, but it was such a curiosity that the diver who found it, Frederick Ingerson, had to open it as soon as he got on deck. To his surprise and the rest of the crew's, this exquisite emerald cross and ring were inside.

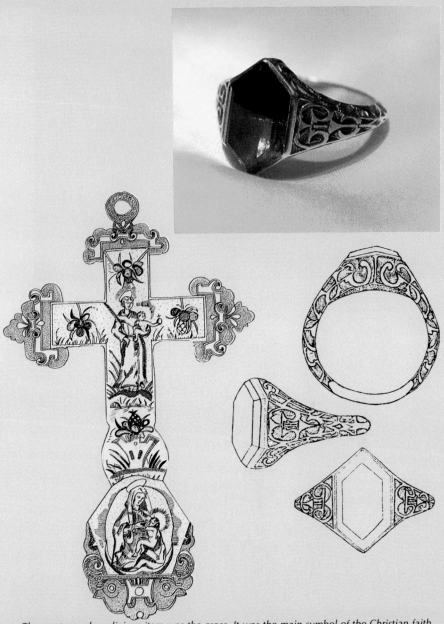

The most popular religious item was the cross. It was the main symbol of the Christian faith and considered a powerful talisman that would bring good fortune to the faithful. The reverse side of this magnificent emerald cross is engraved with the image of a saint and the Madonna holding the Christ child.

Rings were associated with love and marriage. At no such time had rings been worn in such number. The devout wore rings bearing emblems of faith. Popes and bishops wore rings as a sign of their authority and their wealth. This cross and ring are part of a set found inside a silver jewelry case recovered from the Atocha. The 65-karat emerald in the cross came from the mine in the Muzo district of Colombia

One of the most stunning rosaries ever recovered from a shipwreck is the one pictured here, from the Atocha site. Fifty-three red coral beads and five gold beads accentuate the 1¼-inch gold crucifix. The rosary measures 11⅝ inches in length.

Red coral from the Mediterranean, China, and India was thought to have magical powers. Its fiery color was fashionable during the 17th century and became widely used in Europe for fine jewelry. The most beautiful red coral came from Sicily.

Gold crosses studded with gems and hanging pearls were also popular during the 17th century.

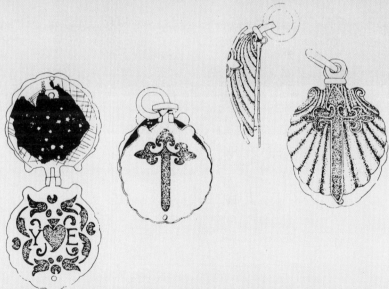

Perhaps no other object found at the Margarita wrecksite illustrates the interplay of gold and enamel and superb craftsmanship than the Santiago pendant, a scalloped-shaped locket found within a large conglomerate. The inner lid of the locket features 13 tiny gold stars set in dark blue enamel. The engravings on the inside and outside are accented with red enamel. The locket remains as new as when the ship went down, although it's slightly bent and does not close properly.

These silver pitchers contained water and wine for communion services. The "V" inscribed on the lid and spout signifies "vino," or wine. A similar pitcher inscribed with an "A" for aqua, or water.

These beautifully crafted silver objects are believed to be salt dispensers. Although not used in religious ceremonies, these pieces reflect the splendid craftsmanship of ecclesiastical silver.

build the device, which they called the "Hydra-Flow," and leased it to him. It was a success. It ripped right through the hardpan down to bedrock. Moved up to the Quicksands, it took less than ten minutes to blow a hole 12 feet deep and 50 feet wide. However, renting the Hydra-Flow was expensive, and it would soon have to be returned. Able to dig fewer holes, we needed better ways to identify anomalies before digging.

Over the next five years, we tried anything and everything that promised results. Our two prime goals were to improve our remote sensing efforts with the magnetometer, sub-bottom sonar, and aerial photography, and improve the accuracy of the positioning of the boats during the search runs.

Finding a position in the middle of the ocean has been a problem—in some ways the preeminent problem—for seafarers since the first man climbed aboard a drifting log and ventured out into open water. Over the centuries, the solutions have become more and more precise. We'd found evidence of that on the *Atocha*: the mariner's astrolabe and brass pocket sundial, crude as they were, were the finest instruments available to the pilots of the 1622 fleet. If their instruments had been better, the Spaniards might have easily located and salvaged the *Atocha* themselves.

The magnetometer could give us readings of promising locations, but if we couldn't come back to that precise spot to investigate, the readings were of little use. Also, if the search runs weren't close enough together, long strips of sea bottom containing artifacts might be missed altogether.

To date, the magnetometer runs had been controlled by observers in towers built up above the surface. Using theodolites—a combination range-finder, direction finder, and telescope—two or more operators radioed the boat captain towing the magnetometer, correcting his course as the "fish," as the magnetometer sensor is called, was pulled through the water. As lanes were searched, they were marked on a nautical chart.

For the theodolite operators, high above the surface in a cramped, open perch, the work was exhausting. The blazing tropical sun baked them, drops of sweat raining onto the instruments and charts as they struggled to concentrate on a tiny, moving dot far across the sea. Errors were inevitable. When the magnetometer found an anomaly, a buoy was thrown over to mark the spot. Later, one of the salvage boats would bring divers to check the area. Too often, these buoys and even the spar buoys we used in the Quicksands area for mapping purposes were cut loose by storm waves or boats passing through.

We were lucky enough to have Dr. Harold Edgerton, emeritus professor at the Massachusetts Institute of Technology who had invented the strobe light, try out one of his inventions on our site. Called a

The brass pocket sundial (above) recovered from the Margarita might have belonged to the navigator or to any of the wealthier passengers. The sunwatch had a compass built into it under the dial so the user would know magnetic north (information necessary for accurate time keeping). Lázaro Fañez de Mineya, a Royal Treasury official from Havana, references pocket sunwatches in his report on the salvage of Margarita by Francisco Nuñez Melián in June 1627.

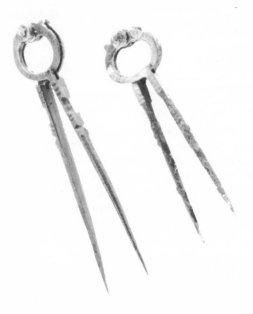

Dividers were used to measure distances on a mariner's chart. The instrument, almost identical to those used today, is hinged at the back. The distance between the tips can be adjusted and used to transfer the distance scale on a map into distance traveled by the ship.

ORIZONTE

This mariner's astrolabe was recovered by Dirk Fisher from the Atocha wrecksite in 1973. Only larger Spanish vessels of a treasure fleet would have carried such an important piece of navigational equipment.

A superficial cleaning revealed the engraved calibration marks. The swivel handle ring at the top was moveable and the alidade, or pointer bar, could pivot on its central pin. This instrument is believed to have belonged to the Atocha's pilot, Martén Jiménez.

The astrolabe was used by mariners to measure the angle of the sun or stars and thus determine the position of the ship relative to its latitude. To calculate a ship's latitude the navigator suspended the astrolabe from his thumb and adjusted it so that the celestial object he was viewing could be sighted through the tiny holes in the vanes. The altitude of the object was then read on a scale of degrees engraved on the wheel-like body of the instrument. Using the angle of delination in conjunction with written tables, the navigator could then establish an estimated latitude.

sub-bottom profiler, it was a new kind of sonar that looked beneath the soft mud or clay on the bottom of the ocean, the way an x-ray reveals bones under a mass of flesh. Yet, almost the whole result of the sub-bottom sonar searches were lost because of missing bouys. Before we brought Fay Feild back to apply his superior knowledge to the magnetometer search, and before we brought back "Doc" Edgerton, we needed a better way to position our boats.

In addition to the human operators in the theodolite towers, in 1977 an ex-Navy commander, Ted Miquel, began helping us install Loran C on our boats. Loran (LOng RAnge Navigation), is an improved version of a technology developed to guide bombers during World War II. A small receiving unit aboard the boat measures the angle between radio transmitters on shore. Multi-digit readouts on the unit correlate to numbers on special Loran C marine charts. Unfortunately, the distance to the government-maintained transmitters and the lack of sensitivity of the receivers gives an accuracy out on the ocean of no better than 50 yards—plenty good enough for finding your way to a mile-long fishing bank, but not nearly good enough for plotting anomalies. Our boats would travel off course during mag runs without seeing any change in the readout on the Loran C unit. This produced large gaps in our overall search pattern.

Still, the technology improved our maps. We still used the surface buoys over the *Atocha* site, but these were tied into our Loran C charts. Both large-scale and small-scale maps could now be made much more quickly. With these more precise artifact maps we were able to learn more about how the ship broke up and its scatter pattern, including details that we'd missed before we'd had the Loran system.

It was becoming clear that, before we could find the motherlode, we had to find a navigational system that would allow us to search huge tracts of ocean bottom quickly and thoroughly. We experimented with the Del Norte navigation system. Much like the Loran system, the Del Norte uses radio signals to determine position. However, the Del Norte's receiver is more sensitive. More important, the Del Norte system comes with its own transmitters, which we set up in two towers. The units on the boats picked up microwave signals from these two transmitters, and a readout gave the distance from each tower. Even in a large area, no two spots will give the same distance reading from the two towers. Plotting the two distances gives the position of the boat, theoretically accurate to within about three feet.

Del Norte produced a revolution in our mapping and search techniques. Syd Jones, who had taken over for Ted Miquel as the captain of the *Swordfish*, spearheaded our experiments with the Del Norte. With it, he was soon able to position the *Swordfish* exactly where he had left off at the end of his last survey trip. The boats were able to hold to their digging patterns, too. If the anchors dragged and the boat moved during a dig, the captains would know it and could reposition the mailboxes exactly where the survey pattern dictated. The holes could be plotted very accurately, ensuring that no large areas of the bottom were missed in our surveys. The captains were able to dig on any exact spot within a ten-square-mile area. When artifacts were found, they could be mapped precisely and these maps merged into maps of the existing scatter pattern, enabling us to extract much more information on the anatomy of the wreck.

Under the guidance of the Del Norte system, the magnetometer runs were accurately placed within a few yards of each other. When an anomaly was found, the coordinates were radioed to the salvage vessels. The salvage vessels then moved in with divers who checked the area while the search boat moved on.

As the weeks progressed, the charts in the maproom seemed to come alive in front of our eyes. In 1981, Ed Little, a marine biologist with mapping experience, joined the company as our chief cartographer. The survey teams kept Ed and his assistants, Peggy Kirwin, Melissa Forte, and Kevin Beede, busy drawing in new details on our maps. New charts appeared, and we felt confident as we plotted search runs and marked finds that we were closing in on the motherlode with ever-increasing accuracy. We'd come a long way from the brass sundials and astrolabes the galleon pilots had used.

While our boats criss-crossed the rolling waters of the Marquesas, we started looking up—straight up. Aerial photography had been used since the 1920s to provide overviews of archaeological sites on land. Could it help us find the motherlode? While Teddy Tucker, a well-known treasure hunter and salvor from Bermuda, and Marty Meylach, a Florida salvor, had both succeeded in spotting treasure wrecks from the air, they'd done it by just visually inspecting an area, not from photographs. They had found their wrecks in shallow, clear water. In the Caribbean, observers in a light airplane can see the details of coral heads under 20 to 40 feet of water. However, the water in Hawk Channel was deeper, and not nearly as clear.

The company had two excellent photographers, Don Kincaid and Pat Clyne. Already, they'd taken a number of aerial photographs that had helped our mapping and survey efforts. Could they now sharpen the technology a bit and find a way to compile clear photomosaics from the air?

Eastman Kodak and the National Aeronautics and Space Administration had developed photographic systems capable of recording intricate bottom detail in deep water. New high-speed color films might give us readings on bottom features in depths up to 60 feet.

Before investing in sophisticated camera systems, however, we stopped to consider how they might be used in the search. They could certainly help us construct a chart showing the location of major bottom features. They might also be able to relocate anomalies that had been discovered in the first side-scan sonar search. The buoys marking these anomalies had been lost in a storm before they were checked. And of course, if our theories about the ballast pile's situation on the bottom were right, we might very well be able to see it in a photograph.

Identifying a hull from a photograph seemed to us to be tricky business. It would involve clues drawn from the photos, rather than simply reviewing thousands of photographs and, one day, shouting "Aha, *there* it is," while looking at a nice, oval ballast pile. We estimated the lower hull was about 60 to 75 feet long and 30 feet wide. In a photo taken from the air, it might show up as a blur a little over a quarter-inch long.

When seen from above, hulls are generally oval in shape. Unfortunately, so are many of the coral patches that litter the bottom of Hawk Channel. The ballast pile itself might even be covered with coral, particularly if it were surrounded with soft sand or mud. In such an area, the ballast pile may be the only hard surface available for marine organisms, such as coral, algae and barnacles, to attach themselves to. After a few centuries, a shipwreck could be a pretty convincing replica of a coral reef.

We'd have to become familiar with the pattern of marine growth in the area and use the photographs to detect areas that looked different, that broke the mold. We suspected there might be a small border separating the ballast pile from the marine growth surrounding it. Natural features, such as rocky outcroppings and reefs, generally are uneven. Anything that looked like a straight line should be checked. Also, when a ship grinds across the top of a coral reef, it kills the coral in its path. The dead coral is white, while the living coral surrounding it is often green or golden-yellow, depending on the species. These white scars can persist for years, and it may be possible to track a vessel's progress through an area by locating such reef scars.

We might also be able to tell something about the texture of bottom materials from the photos. The artifacts would probably reflect light somewhat differently than the natural materials surrounding them. These differences would be evident from slight differences in tone and color value on the photos.

The photos might let us construct depth-contour maps more quickly than other survey methods, such as sonar. These maps would give us some clues as to what the shipwreck would look like in specific areas based on the bottom features and depth.

We knew that, for the photos to be useful, we'd have to become experts at interpreting the images. We'd have to learn to recognize the photographic "signature" of a rocky outcropping, a bed of coral, a patch of sand or mud, before we could recognize shipwreck material.

Finally, the photos had to be taken with a high degree of locational accuracy so that they could be tied into our magnetometer searches, sonar searches, exploratory digging, and artifact scatter maps. It would give us yet another way of looking at our search area, a way that tied the "blind" data we were getting from our electronic instruments to clear, visual images.

We decided to test and develop an aerial survey, but before it could be launched, some unexpected news from an area east of the *Atocha* sited derailed our plans.

chapter 9

A Priceless Treasure

Throughout 1978 and 1979, we had continued to make scattered finds in the Quicksands. The *James Bay*, another salvage boat, was brought in and her captain and crew worked as subcontractors, combing the Quicksands. A number of excellent artifacts came up and a great deal of treasure as well. These were telling us volumes about life aboard the ship but very little new information as to where the main part of the *Atocha* might be.

In January 1980, Mel held a meeting with the boat captains and crews to discuss what should be done next. While everyone wanted to concentrate on finding the *Atocha*, we had yet to locate the ballast trail that led out into Hawk Channel. The boats had dug the search corridor again and again, trying in vain to pick up traces of the scatter of ballast and artifacts leading out from the bronze cannons found by Dirk Fisher in 1975. We knew the trail had to be there—but why couldn't we pick it up?

Despite all of the evidence that the hull was in deep water to the southeast—the identification of the Quicksands scatter as parts of the sterncastle, the meteorological information, Gene's historical research—there was a growing feeling in the company that the main part of the wreck lay to the northwest of the anchor, farther up in the Quicksands. Many members of the salvage crew felt our efforts should be concentrated in that direction. While we were recovering treasure in the Quicksands, treasure that helped make the payroll and keep the company alive, it wasn't providing any new clues to the location of the motherlode. What we needed was not more treasure trickling in, but solid scientific evidence.

Over the years, when new clues were needed, we'd often gotten them from Gene Lyon's Spanish documents. Once again, Mel began reviewing these papers with Gene and others. Just as the *Virgilona* and *Swordfish* had methodically dug the Quicksands for clues, Mel and Gene dug through the sometimes contradictory accounts of the sinking of the 1622 fleet. The most complete information, of course, concerned the *Margarita*. Sixty-eight of the 194 people aboard had survived, and the site had been salvaged periodically by the Spanish for almost 20 years. Mel and others in the company began to think more about the *Margarita*. Despite the Spanish salvage efforts, a large amount of silver and gold should still remain on the site. With the better historical documentation, might it be easier to find than the *Atocha*?

The best piece of evidence Gene had found was the eyewitness account of Captain Bernardino de Lugo. As the *Margarita* was driven up into the shallows, he had seen the *Atocha* sinking about three miles to the east. But other documents placed the *Atocha* west of the *Margarita*. Now that we had a positive identification on the general area of the *Atocha's* wrecksite, we had a place to begin looking for the *Margarita*. But was it east or west?

The area to the east had already been surveyed extensively by Continental Exploration, the organization run by Burt Webber, John Berrier, Richard MacAllaster, and Jack Haskins. After Treasure Salvors had made its first finds in the Quicksands in 1971, these four had been granted state permits to look for the galleons in the area east of the anchor find. They were experienced salvors. They ran very systematic searches and their magnetometer techniques were highly developed. Some of the Treasure Salvors people felt that, if there were anything in the area east of the Quicksands, Webber and his group would have found it.

Still, the historical record wasn't clear as to which direction was correct, and there was no clear consensus among the salvage crew. In February and March, the *Swordfish* and the *Virgilona* began to search both east and west of the *Atocha* area.

Hoping for a quicker find, Mel hired a subcontractor, Bobby Jordan, to bring a boat and crew into the search for the *Margarita*. Working the area to the east, in March 1980 Jordan recovered a small anchor, a large copper cauldron, a number of pottery fragments, some indigo dyestuff, and clumps of silver coins.

Immediately, we began trying to understand these finds. When the eight *reale* coins were cleaned, we found they were minted in the reign of Philip III. Almost certainly they had come from the 1622 fleet, but from which ship? Were they part of the *Atocha* scatter? Did they come from the *Margarita*? Or were they the remains of one of the smaller merchant ships that had sunk in the 1622 storm?

Don Kincaid took the lead in plotting the location of the artifacts as they were recovered. As he worked with Ed Little and Melissa Forte, our cartographers, an artifact scatter pattern began to emerge in the company's maproom. The trail led north.

Working in that direction, three gold bars were soon recovered in an area surrounded by ballast, potsherds, and other shipwreck debris. The largest bar sent shock waves through the company: It was 11 inches long and weighed almost five pounds!

The *Virgilona* and the *Swordfish* converged on the artifact trail. Soon they were recovering a myriad of items: potsherds, bones, lead sheathing barrel hoops, and spikes. On April 12, two more gold bars came up. The crews raced, each vying to find the main site, to bring up more gold, more artifacts than the others. After long years of working the thin scatter of artifacts on the *Atocha* site, here was a reason to get excited. Throughout May, finds continued to pour in: hundreds of silver coins, silver plates, swords, arquebuses, and a fragmented mariner's astrolabe. As the month progressed it became evident that this was not a small merchant vessel. The large quantity of weapons indicated that this was a capital ship. The *Atocha* site lay approximately three miles to the west. It had to be the *Margarita*.

There was very little question about the wreck, but we had to be absolutely sure. As we had done with the *Atocha* site, we needed to link the physical evidence, the artifacts from the site, to the historical records to irrefutably date and identify the wreck as the *Margarita*. Critics were waiting for Treasure Salvors to make a mistake. Mel's competitors were in the wings, hoping for a chance to salvage the galleons. State and federal authorities were watching every move. Academic archaeologists were crying to the press, claiming we were raping and pillaging an irreplaceable cultural treasure. However, instead of acting carelessly as they believed treasure hunters acted, we worked very, very carefully. We knew this wreck was a major discovery, and that it could rival what had already been done on the *Atocha*. Everyone was determined to excavate it properly.

As soon as it was apparent we had the right vicinity Mel filed an Admiralty lawsuit in the U.S. District Court for the Southern District of Florida in Miami. Over the years, a variety of courts had struck down claims by the State of Florida and the U.S. Federal Government that they owned the site of the *Atocha*, and therefore had jurisdiction over it. When the smoke cleared, the result of the court rulings was that, after years of confusion and bitter feuding, the judges had decided that shipwrecks inside state waters as well as outside fall under the provisions of Admiralty Law.

Admiralty is a collection of court decisions that has evolved gradually over the past three or four centuries, first in English courts, then American. The U.S. Constitution gives Admiralty Law exclusive jurisdiction over anything that happens on the open seas; commerce and shipping, accidents, and the like. When the U.S. courts ruled against the State and the Federal Government, they in effect said that the laws upon which their claims were based didn't apply to shipwrecks. In looking for some established body of legal tradition to use in their rulings, the courts fell back on Admiralty, which offered a well-defined procedure for granting a legal title to own an abandoned shipwreck.

Shipwrecks are owned by the person or company who held the title to the ship before it sank. If that owner can't be found, as in the case of an unidentified, 350-year-old galleon, anyone who finds the wreck can file a lawsuit asking a Federal Court to give them the legal title. The court assumes jurisdiction of the wreck. In most cases, the court designates the person who filed the lawsuit as the salvor in possession of the wreck. As the cargo and other materials are recovered, the court can direct who should receive the materials. The court can also place conditions on the salvor—it may require a monetary bond be posted, or that the salvage be carried out in an archaeological manner. The salvor gains two advantages. First, he receives a clear, indisputable legal title to the salvaged material remitted to him by the court. Second, no other salvors are allowed to work the wrecksite. If anyone tries to horn in, they can be arrested. The courts can then, if they choose, jail the interlopers for as long as seems appropriate to the judge.

The *Atocha* site had been handled in this way, and Treasure Salvors had been designated as the salvor in possession of the wreck by the U.S. District Court for the Southern District of Florida. As long as the company continued its archaeological work on the site, the court would protect Mel's claim on the wreck.

After warding off threats from the outside for so long, Mel was now surprised to find he had a claim jumper in his own organization. After the admiralty suit had been filed in Miami, Bobby Jordan hit a big strike. His crew recovered more than 50 pounds of gold bullion and disks, and Jordan caught gold fever.

Jordan and his backers had worked out a secret radio code, and after hauling up the gold, Jordan called them. The call let them know that he wouldn't be returning to Key West. Then he put his plan into action.

Mel had placed a diver, R.D. LeClair, on Jordan's boat to monitor the salvage operation. Jordan pulled into Key West harbor and dropped anchor, waiting for a signal from shore. When LeClair tried to use the radio to inform Treasure Salvors of the fabulous find, Jordan warned him away from the microphone, as he strapped on a revolver, LeClair was stunned. He knew that Jordan was hijacking Mel's gold, and whether Jordan planned to run for open water or dock elsewhere in the Keys, LeClair knew Jordan wouldn't let him go to tell his story.

On shore, Don Kincaid noticed Jordan's boat in the harbor. He thought that strange because Jordan hadn't contacted the Key West office for several days. Suddenly, Jordan pulled anchor and took off at high speed. Now, Don knew something was up.

Jordan docked near Summerland Key, and was met by a U.S. Marshal. Jordan told the marshal that he'd found a shipwreck and was filing an Admiralty claim. Following the correct procedure, the marshall "arrested" the site, placing it under the jurisdiction of the Federal District Court pending settlement of Jordan's claim.

The merriment didn't last long. Almost as quickly as the theft was accomplished, the problem was solved. Mel's attorney, David Horan, informed the District Court that Jordan had been under contract to Treasure Salvors and that the gold had been recovered from the site that the Court had already granted to Treasure Salvors.

The court in Miami immediately transferred the gold found by Jordan to Treasure Salvors, but the legal battle continued for two years. Eventually, the court denied Jordan's suit for ownership and denied him a share of the treasure, ruling that he'd acted in bad faith. As so often happens in treasure hunting, a dizzying high quickly turned into a personal tragedy.

Ironically, during the planning of this scam, Jordan lived next door to me on Little Torch Key. The subdivision was called Jolly Roger Estates, and we lived just a block off Pirate's Road.

With the Jordan affair settled, Mel now had to contend with another group of claim jumpers. Even after losing the *Atocha* case, at a high cost to the state's taxpayers, the State of Florida once again intervened, this time claiming ownership of the *Margarita*. While Mel and Dave Horan worked diligently to protect the site, we applied ourselves to studying the artifacts, trying to glean as many clues as possible to the location of the bulk of the *Margarita* material.

I once again impressed on the divers that the artifacts they were recovering weren't just a random group of objects, each was part of a pattern. The material recovered to date had been scattered thinly over the bedrock in a wide area. We had to put as much information as possible on our maps. If we could discern the pattern, it would lead us to the main site of the wreck.

By comparing the ship's manifest to the salvage reports submitted by Melián, we learned what artifacts to expect. The manifest showed that the ship had carried 419 silver ingots; 118,000 silver coins; 1,488 ounces of gold in 34 bars or disks; and copper ingots, silverware, tobacco, and indigo. Undoubtedly, there was a great load of gold aboard that wasn't listed on the manifest; contraband being smuggled to Spain to avoid the *quinto* tax. Melián's salvage had brought up over 350 silver ingots, of which 67 were untaxed contraband. This led us to believe there was far more treasure remaining on the site.

Don Kincaid, Kane Fisher, Tom Ford, and Syd Jones pitched in to help solve the archaeological questions. As captain of the *Swordfish*, Syd Jones continued to explore the area north of Jordan's find. Throughout June 1980 the *Virgilona* found more scattered fragments until, suddenly, they hit a rich pocket of artifacts. Kane Fisher, who had spotted the first silver ingots from the *Atocha* in 1973, saw it first. While swimming over the search area, he found six silver ingots resting out in the open on bedrock in two neatly-spaced rows. Nearby, he spotted a pile of ballast stones, copper ingots, and clumps containing thousands of silver coins. Even more exciting to me was what lay beneath this wealthy pile. All around the bottom, we could see wooden planks from the lower hull of the ship. After a decade of digging we had finally recovered part of the wooden hull of the 1622 galleon.

The *Swordfish* quickly came in to join the *Virgilona* in systematically surveying the area around the ballast pile. The crews were instructed to map every artifact, no matter how small, before it was moved. After the site had been thoroughly surveyed, we carefully removed the ballast covering the hull.

This virgin pile of shipwreck debris was a wonderful sight. The piece of wooden hull was 23 feet long; a web of wooden ribs and planking supporting a heap of artifacts and ballast, including a 105-pound mass of silver coins fused together in the shape of a wooden chest. There was no doubt that this was the major remains of the *Margarita*. Of course, our critics weren't going to take our word for it. We'd need proof.

Once again, we turned to the historical records to tie together the physical evidence from the wrecksite with the 17th century Spanish accounts documenting the ship, the wreck, and the salvage efforts. Of the first six silver ingots found by Kane, Gene matched the markings of five precisely with the *Margarita's* manifest. Of the dated coins, none dated later than 1622. The wide array of weapons and personal effects was overwhelming; no one could doubt the identity of this wreck.

With the credibility of the company—with the press, with the Federal Court overseeing the salvage, with investors—riding on their handling of the *Margarita*, the divers pitched in to help with the archaeology. It was soon obvious that the artifacts spread out in a narrow pattern to the north, stretching out from the hull. About 300 yards north, a bronze cannon was found. Then a second. Then an anchor. Then a mass of artifacts fused together—cannonballs, personal effects, pieces of the shipwreck. As we worked and mapped these finds, the drama of the *Margarita's* sinking unfolded.

A large grid was made out of plastic pipe to help us map the structure and the finds. A baseline was laid down along the middle of the hull and basic measurements were taken to give us a three-dimensional perspective of the whole site. With that complete, the grid was laid over the hull. Each timber was numbered and lettered. Pat Clyne had built a camera track that fit over the plastic grid. By moving the camera along the track, he would be able to take a series of slightly overlapping photos. These would be merged into one giant print, giving us a photomosaic of the entire hull structure.

We wanted as many types of photographic images of the hull as possible, and a variety of underwater photographic experts were invited to assist us. Ray McAllister, a professor of Ocean Engineering from Florida Atlantic University, agreed to help. So did Dmitri Rebikoff, an engineer and inventor who had worked with Jacques Cousteau in the 1950s. Rebikoff had invented a lens which corrected the distortion that affected ordinary camera lenses when used underwater. He brought his *Pegasus*—a combination diver propulsion vehicle and camera—out to the site. The *Pegasus* resembles a self-propelled torpedo with a survey camera in the nose. A diver rides the *Pegasus*, steering it over the bottom as the camera takes sequential, overlapping photos. These can later be merged into a single photomosaic of the entire site.

The level of expertise brought to the site by these professionals underlined the importance we attached to the recovery of the *Margarita*'s hull. It was one of the largest pieces of an early wooden hull that had been studied anywhere in the Americas. We had a responsibility to do as precise a job as possible, gathering the data that would allow other researchers to compare these remains with others that had been found in the Western Hemisphere. I was particularly interested in comparing the *Margarita*'s hull with that of the *San Juan*, a Basque whaler recovered by Canadian archaeologists in Labrador. The *San Juan*, launched about 1560, had been built in the same city as the *Margarita*, in Viscayon region along Spain's north coast. Comparing the hulls might provide new insights into the evolution of Spanish galleons. The *San Juan* had been built just before the defeat of the Spanish Armada by the English in 1588. The *Margarita* had been built a generation afterward. By studying each timber carefully, measuring its fasteners, examining each part of the planking, it might be possible to look into the minds of the Spanish shipwrights, to see how they had altered the design of ships subsequent to the greatest sea battle of that period.

While we studied the timbers, careful digging revealed an enormous number of gold bars and chains. Pat Clyne and Don Kincaid, working with the crew of the *Swordfish*, brought up 15 chains totalling 34 feet long within a small area. On August 23, Syd Jones made a spectacular discovery. While snorkeling, he spotted nine gold bars and eight chains lying close together on bare bedrock.

No one had ever seen such a concentration of gold bars and chains as this wreck was yielding. The efforts of the entire company were turned to the *Margarita*, and over the next 18 months, the wreck gave up 43 chains, totaling about 180 feet in length. Each chain was different, each carefully wrought of exquisitely handcrafted links. Don Kincaid observed that the *Margarita* should be called the "Gold Chain Wreck," and the name stuck. A London auction house speculated the finds might be worth $40 million or more.

While the attention of the press focused on the spectacular treasure, I was absorbed by new archaeological questions raised by the artifacts we'd recovered. Why was there so much chain here? Was it made by Indian goldsmiths working under the supervision of Spaniards? Was it gold being shipped back to Spain in the guise of personal jewelry in order to avoid paying the *quinto* tax?

Our research staff was invigorated by these fresh questions. The *Margarita* site contained a far wider range of objects than the pieces of the *Atocha* found to date. We'd found the lid to an ivory box, carved with depictions of mythical animals. It had probably come from Ceylon or India, shipped to Acapulco on the Manila galleon and transported across Mexico to Vera Cruz. It had come 10,000 miles across the Pacific Ocean and wound up here in the Florida Keys, mixed with Colombian emeralds in a profusion of settings, masses of coins, and a gold boatswain's whistle. A brass pocket sundial was found as well. The pocketwatch was still years in the future when the owners of these crude, though beautifully-made, timepieces drowned.

While working off the *Virgilona*, Dick Klaudt discovered an eight-inch plate made of solid gold, its surface covered with intricate designs reminiscent of 15th-century Moorish motifs. Nothing like this plate had been found on a shipwreck anywhere in the Americas or anywhere in the world. Scholars from several museums in Western Europe feel that the plate is the most unique object recovered from the *Margarita*.

A larger conservation team had been built gradually to treat and preserve artifacts as they came up. Jim Sinclair, a recent graduate of Franklin Pierce College, had joined us in February 1980 as an archaeologist and immediately began work to expand our Key West Lab. Although it was initially little more than a first aid station, where artifacts could be stabilized before being treated for permanent preservation elsewhere, it soon expanded. Claudia Linzee, who had been working for the company for some time, recorded finds and cataloged material as it came in from the site. Her background in art history made her very sensitive to the meaning and care of the artifacts. Curt Peterson, and Austin Fowles, two of the best shipwreck conservators in America helped us improve the facilities and techniques. They had worked for the State of Florida, running their conservation lab in Tallahassee, and were already very familiar with the *Atocha* materials. Jerry Cash, a diver, sailor, and professional artist, was helping map the hull structure and artifacts on the site, Bill Muir, a draftsman and self-taught ship historian, not only drew the *Margarita* timbers from our site maps, photos, and measurements, but began researching the *Atocha* contract that Gene had found. Using information from the *Margarita* timbers and from Gene's research, he began drawings that would show us wnat the *Atocha* had looked like.

The ballast had been carefully moved off the timbers to

permit measurements and photographs. Now, as we completed our study of the hull, Don Kincaid remarked on how clean the ballast was. The surfaces of the rocks were mostly free of barnacles and other marine growth that ordinarily fastens on to any exposed surface in the ocean. Kincaid suggested that, although Kane Fisher had found the pile sitting right out in the open, that it may have been covered by sand until very recently. Just before the pile was found, the area had been struck by several storms. It's possible that the wave surge kicked up by the storms had uncovered the *Margarita*, allowing us to find it. Our boats had been dragging magnetometers over the area for months, yet had missed the pile. We also knew that Jack Haskins and John Berrier had concentrated their search in this area a few years earlier when they held claims surrounding Mel's *Atocha* claim. They were careful, methodical shipwreck salvors. Why had they missed it? The sea is capricious. Perhaps Haskins and Berrier had missed the *Margarita* simply because it was buried in deep sand. When asked, Haskins and Berrier told us they had often anchored for the night in the area where we found the *Margarita's* hull. It became a standing joke in the company that Jack and John had actually found the *Margarita* years ago, but hadn't known enough to look over the side. As Mel had proved over the years, shipwreck archaeology isn't all science—it takes luck as well as logic.

oins

Hand-held metal detectors are used at close range to find small pieces of metal, such as clumps of coins. Approximately 250,000 silver coins of various denominations were aboard the Atocha; two years' output of the Royal Mints at Potosi, Lima, Mexico City, Santa Fe de Bogota, and Santiago de Chile. Historians estimate that the value of these coins, when recovered and cleaned of the grime accumulated over three centuries underwater, could total between $46 million and $115 million dollars.

Silver coins from the Atocha. These coins were minted in Santa Fe de Bogota.

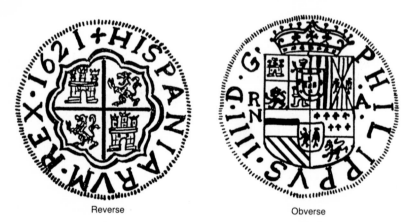

Reverse   Obverse

Although there were nearly a quarter-million coins on the Atocha, 12 identical silver "pieces–of–eight," (Markings above) are the rarest and most important yet found.

These were the first issue of the mint at Santa Fe de Bogota, struck during the few months the mint operated in 1621. Historians have long known that the Bogota mint was operational in 1621, but none of the coins minted that year had been seen until these were found on the Atocha site. Markings on the coins reveal the mint, the assayer or mintmaster and the date of issue. The front (obverse) of the coins carries the shield of the powerful Hapsburg family which ruled the Holy Roman Empire, including Spain; the name of the reigning king, Philip IV (shown as IIII); the letters "D G," or Deo Gloria; the legend "RN" indicating they were minted at Bogota in Nuevo Reino de Grenada province; and an "A" signifying the mintmaster of that period, Alonso Turillo de Yebra.

The back of the coins (reverse) is emblazoned with the Lion of the province of Leon and the Castle representing Castille—the two powerful regions that united to form the kingdom of Spain—within a Crusader's Cross. This side was also marked with the legend "Hispaniarum Rex," or "Spain rules," and the date.

Coins provide vital evidence in the dating of shipwrecks. These coins (top) were minted in Seville, Spain in 1621, one year before the wreck. Gold coins were not regularly minted in the New World until 1679, and none were listed as cargo on the Atocha's manifest. These coins, found on the site of the Margarita, were probably the pocket change of a wealthy passenger.

The coat of arms of the Great House of Hapsburg reflected the vast dominions of that family, which ruled Spain and a number of other European countries during the 16th and 17th centuries. The insignia was divided into four basic quadrants, and these were subdivided as new territories were added.

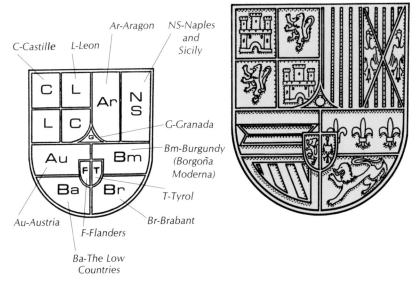

Ar-Aragon

NS-Naples and Sicily

C-Castille L-Leon

C   L   Ar   N
S
L   C

G-Granada

Au   Bm   Bm-Burgundy (Borgoña Moderna)

F T

Ba   Br   T-Tyrol

Au-Austria

Br-Brabant

F-Flanders

Ba-The Low Countries

The Atocha's manifest shows she was carrying about 250,000 coins. After three centuries underwater, many of them are covered with a thick layer of silver oxide. Others have been cemented together, such as this large clump of coins found on the motherlode site fused into the shape of the coin chest they were shipped in.

chapter 10

The Motherlode

While crews continued to work the *Margarita* site, I turned my attention back to the *Atocha*. The *Margarita* had given all of us new energy, and had brought in needed investments to keep the search moving. For two long years, we concentrated on picking signs of shipwreck scatter leading from the bronze cannons out to Hawk Channel. Hundreds of magnetic and side-scan sonar anomalies were recorded and evaluated but they produced little results.

There were few finds to break the monotony of surveying and diving. The most exciting of these came in the summer of 1981. Bob Moran and the crew of the *Plus Ultra* located three anchors in about 40 feet of water just inside the Outer Reef. Two of the anchors had well-preserved wooden stocks and the other one had foundry and weight marks inscribed alongside the date "1618." We believed these had been hooked into the reef in a last-ditch attempt to keep the *Atocha* from tearing her bottom out on the jagged coral ledge.

Shortly after this find, another search boat located an iron bar, pointed at one end, that measured more than six feet long. It closely resembled the wrecking bar mentioned in a 1623 account of the Spanish salvage attempts. Though many questions remained to be answered about this latest find, the dramatic new discovery indicated that we were in the right area and were getting closer to the motherlode.

In 1982 Kane Fisher, who'd found the first silver ingot in the Bank of Spain almost ten years before, became captain of his own boat, the *Dauntless*. Like his older brother, Dirk, Kane was convinced that the main deposit was somewhere in the deeper water of Hawk Channel. Though almost everyone else in the company still believed it was up in the shallow Quicksands, Kane tenaciously stuck to our deep water theory.

For the next two-and-one half years, Kane and his crew on the *Dauntless* followed the treasure trail out into Hawk Channel. In the beginning, the finds were sparse—a few ballast stones, iron nails, and small encrusted objects. But it was a start. Just as the tiny musketball found up in the Quicksands had convinced Mel a decade before, these small objects told us we were near the *Atocha*. For the first time, there was concrete evidence of *Atocha* material in the middle of Hawk Channel. As the search continued, the *Virgilona* and *Swordfish* crews helped close in on the scatter pattern. When something was found, their spirits were high. But when days would go by without a single find—not even rock ballast—frustration set in. When their morale reached its lowest point, many crew members abandoned the deep water theory and returned to the Quicksands area and the Bank of Spain. The gold bars and silver coins found here refueled their enthusiasm, but they didn't bring us any closer to finding the motherlode.

Then in 1984 Fay Feild made a spectacular discovery. While helping Bob Moran set up a remote sensing survey of the area north of the Bank of Spain he spotted a beautiful bronze cannon lying right out in the open. This was the first cannon from the *Atocha* site we had found in the Quicksands. Careful digging produced a number of small ship's artifacts and another extraordinary find—two large galleon anchors that were also identified to the *Atocha*. What did this all mean? Just when we were closing in on an all-out assault in Hawk Channel, we now had signs that the big treasure might be in the Quicksands area after all. The company was now divided more than ever about where to look for the motherlode.

In March 1985, Mel decided for an all-out search effort to pick up the scattered trail of material which Kane had been following in Hawk Channel. *Saba Rock*, a new 167-foot salvage vessel captained by Jim Duran joined the hunt. Earlier, she had been digging in the Quicksands with some success. Chip Clemmons and the crew of his survey boat, the *Bookmaker*, had picked up several barrel hoops with the magnetometer. This and other finds by the *Dauntless*—spikes and small rock ballast—added small, but significant, pieces to the puzzle.

As the 1985 diving season opened, the trail just petered out. Something had to be done to pick it up again. Throughout April, the *Saba Rock* dug one hole after another; all of them bone dry. Then, the boat moved to a new area which immediately started to produce some ballast. Later I saw Ed Stevens, the new captain of the *Saba Rock*. He and his fiancee, Susan Nelson, were grinning from ear to ear. They proudly showed me their important find—a 20-pound ballast rock. They both shared my feeling that ballast would eventually lead us to the gold. I knew that it was only a matter of time before a major find would be made along the trail toward the southeast.

The find we all anxiously awaited came over the Memorial Day weekend. Susan Nelson was the first to spot it. There on the bottom was a glittering cashe of treasure: 13 gold bars; 414 silver coins; 4 finely detailed gold pieces of jewelry mounted with 16 emeralds; and assorted pieces of silverware. Now we had more than ballast and barrel hoops to show for our work in Hawk Channel.

Mel immediately went out to the site to congratulate the divers. He urged them to search the area thoroughly, and carefully record exactly where they found each artifact. Before he left, he joked with the divers, telling them to be sure to find more emeralds. Mel had always believed that a large shipment of uncut emeralds had been smuggled on board the *Atocha*. Though he claimed he'd seen documents proving this illicit shipment many years ago, the historical evidence had never surfaced. Mel's story about how the emeralds came to be secretly stashed on board was intriguing. But like most treasure stories, it was difficult to separate fact from fantasy.

The next day, diving off the *Saba Rock*, K. T. Budde-Jones and her husband, Syd Jones, found exactly what Mel had asked for—uncut emeralds. This was the first group of many exquisite emeralds that would be revealed along other parts of the trail. Mel's emerald story had become far more real than anyone could have imagined.

The divers morale soared, but once again, after weeks of digging, the trail ran out. Mel directed Kane to take the *Dauntless* further down the line to the southeast to investigate areas that Ed Little, our cartographer, thought might produce signs of the trail. Earlier magnetometer surveys and our work with the side-scan sonar had registered several anomalies that might tie in with the shipwreck scatter found on Memorial Day weekend. Meanwhile, the *Swordfish*, captained by Tom Ford began exploring anomalies picked up by the magnetometer about a half mile southeast of the Memorial Day site. Digging in this area revealed an iron breech-loading swivel gun, cannon shot, rigging and other residue of the *Atocha's* upper superstructure.

On Wednesday, July 16, the *Dauntless* uncovered a heavy concentration of artifacts near one of the anomalies picked up during a magnetometer survey. Soon, copper, ingots, ballast, and thousands of silver coins were uncovered on the sea bed. This was the major discovery that we had anticipated for more than five years. When Mel called me from the wrecksite, he could hardly contain his excitement. "Kane has just found a whole bunch of treasure and ballast. How about that!" Mel exclaimed. "I think we've really found it this time."

The next day, Don Kincaid and I took a speed boat out to the site to find out what had happened since Mel's call. When we climbed on board the *Dauntless*, the crew began talking all at once, pointing out what they'd discovered. The ship pulsed from the thrust of the mailboxes, which were running at full speed. As I talked to Kane Fisher, the

The mortar and pestle were probably used by the ship's surgeon. The surgeon carried an assortment of herbs and other medicinal substances including chinaroot, sarsaparilla, henna, mercury, and quaiacum. The mortar and pestle were used to grind the herbs, while the set of weights were used to measure the ingredients. Sickness was rife on early sea voyages, with scurvy, dysentery, smallpox, and syphilis claiming victims along with the more common seasickness.

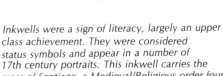

Inkwells were a sign of literacy, largely an upper class achievement. They were considered status symbols and appear in a number of 17th century portraits. This inkwell carries the cross of Santiago, a Medieval/Religious order founded in 1175. The center of the well held a small glass or ceramic ink container. The smaller holes at each corner held the quills.

This sand shaker and candlestick were indispensable tools aboard ship. The shaker held sand, used to help dry ink on a log entry or documents after writing.

Very little light penetrated below decks, so that lanterns and candles were necessary despite the danger of fire.

crew kept bringing up more artifacts. In a matter of a day, they had recovered thousands of silver coins, copper ingots, ornate silverware, and some fascinating rigging. The chain plates and long drift pins suggested to me that we were very close to, if not right on top of, the motherlode.

But we were still missing some major artifacts. We needed to find the stacks of silver ingots and chests of coins that were recorded on the *Atocha*'s manifest. We knew the galleon had carried as many as 60 coin chests when she went down. Kane kidded me about my hesitancy to tag his wonderful discovery as the *Atocha*'s motherlode. Andy Matroci, one of the archaeological recorders who had been involved in the search for several years, was eager to know what I thought. As Andy and the rest of Kane's crew crowded around, I knew I was in a difficult position. The last thing I wanted to do was downplay their discovery, a significant one at that. But I still couldn't ignore the absence of the large ballast, coin chests, stacked silver ingots, ship timbers, and pottery.

I explained to the crew that we had to be careful about identifying this site as part of the *Atocha* until we were absolutely sure. Too much was at stake to make an early announcement that we might have to retract. The company had cried "wolf" several times in the past in its rush to tell the world about the marvelous discoveries. This time, we hoped to be absolutely certain of the identification before going to the media. Our critics would love for us to incorrectly identify the wrecksite. Of course, if this wasn't the *Atocha* what could it be? We had no records of other ships sinking in the area with this much treasure aboard.

The lack of certain artifacts had played a major role in identifying the *Atocha*'s sterncastle in the Quicksands. Years ago, when we didn't locate the cannons and anchors there, we directed our search to Hawk Channel. That realization haunted me as I studied the artifacts laid out on the deck of the *Dauntless*. Not only were a number of key artifacts missing, but our geographic location didn't jibe at all with my expectations. We were situated a full three miles from the most recent *Atocha* find that lined up with the anchor, bronze cannon, and ballast trail. In fact, the site was much more closely aligned with the main scatter of the *Margarita* site, which lay three miles north. Maybe the divers had found a cluster of material that spilled out as the *Margarita* bounced along the bottom before arriving at her final grave in the Quicksands.

As divers celebrated on deck, I helped Andy compile the artifact inventory. We assigned individual tag numbers to each find and entered them into the ship's log. Over the years Andy had developed into a reliable archaeological recorder, and I was glad he was able to share in many exciting moments of discovery, particularly now. As I pressed him for more details about what he had seen on the bottom, the radio crackled in the wheelhouse. Bleth McHaley was calling from home base. She wanted to know what I thought about the discovery and what information she should pass along to the press.

"I'm going to have to tell the newspapers something." Bleth said. "What do you think? The people at *National Geographic* want to know what's going on, but I don't want to notify them prematurely."

I hesitated before answering. "Bleth, this a terrific find, but I can't really say it's the *Atocha* without more proof. Maybe we should hold off for a few days to give Kane and his divers more time to explore the site." She agreed that this was the best approach. Until more archaeological data was gathered, the news of the discovery would be withheld.

As Don and I started our journey back to the Key West office, I tried to sort the questions that had to be answered before we could positively identify this site as the *Atocha*. I immediately thought of Gene Lyon. His research in Seville had played such a major role in the search for the galleons. Now that we were so close, I wondered how he would react to this new find.

Beer and conversation flowed freely as Don Kincaid guided the boat to Key West. Everybody had a theory about Kane's discovery. I tried to relax and enjoy the experience, but I kept thinking about the incredible amount of archaeological work that would have to be done if this was the *Atocha*'s motherlode.

Ten years before, when it appeared we were close to finding the galleon, I had prepared an elaborate archaeological plan for identifying and preserving the *Atocha*'s riches. Now I didn't even know where to start looking for those old files.

That was only part of my concern. Ten years before, I had been mentally prepared to bring up the motherlode. I wasn't quite sure I was ready for that responsibility now. I'd have to get everyone at Treasure Salvors to work together. There was only one *Atocha* in the whole universe. If we dismembered this wonderful time capsule without carefully recording all the artifacts, we would permanently destroy an extraordinary historical treasure. Did I have the mental and physical energy to push everyone in the company hard enough to get the work done right? Was the crew experienced enough to handle the job responsibly? Would I be able to attract professional archaeologists to the project? The closer we got to Key West, the more I doubted my abilities. With the closing act of this great drama staring me in the face, I nearly choked with stage fright.

That night, instead of going back to my house on Little Torch Key, I stayed in Key West. I arrived at Treasure Salvor's office early the next day. Though it was only 8 A.M., Bleth was already on the phone talking excitedly about our discovery. We still hadn't released an official statement, but no doubt this would happen soon. An investor with $1 million to put into the company was negotiating with Mel. Their conversation paused only to listen to reports of more finds coming over the radio.

By now, Kane was absolutely convinced that we had the *Atocha*. New finds were continually reported—more coins, more copper ingots, more ballast. But still no hull timbers or silver ingots. Everyone had caught treasure fever except me. Sensing my skepticism, Bleth got off the phone and turned her chair toward me.

"When will you be satisfied?" she asked. It was obvious that everyone was growing impatient. But I had a professional responsibility to myself, to the *Atocha*, and to the company, to be right.

My reply was cautious. "As soon as we find the silver ingots stacked one on top of the other, then there will be no question that we've found the motherlode."

Wendy Tucker, assistant editor for the *Key West Citizen*, had been reporting on the search for over a decade. She wanted to file a story immediately and get an announcement out to the wire services.

"We probably have it, but an announcement would be premature," I said, trying to sound hopeful. "Let's just wait a little longer. I'm sure that the *Dauntless* will bring up the news we've all been waiting for."

There was no other way for me to respond, no matter how much it dampened the treasure hunters' spirits. This wreck would rewrite the textbook on shipwreck archaeology. It had to be done right.

I paced the office, hoping I was doing the right thing. Bleth and Wendy wanted to break the story. Mel was convinced that we had found the *Atocha*. But then, he had been certain of this many times in the past. As for Kane, well, no amount of archaeological protocol would change his spirit. His youth and exuberance overrode everything else.

At the instant that thought passed through my mind, Kane's voice came over the radio. "Put away the charts. We found it!"

Although Kane sounded calm and self-assured, I was certain that the scene aboard the *Dauntless* was total bedlam. Andy Matroci and Greg Wareham had just swum into a huge stack of silver ingots. The mountain of silver that we had earnestly sought for the past 16 years was finally ours. Today, July 20, 1985, was finally the day. At the time, no one realized the significance of the date: ten years to the day after the *Northwind* capsized, killing Dirk, Angel, and Rick Gage. It was Dirk's find of the *Atocha* cannons which linked the trail of artifacts from the Quicksands with those in deeper water and eventually led us to the motherlode.

Almost immediately everyone wanted to dive on the treasure. The water visibility wasn't good, and a thin layer of sand covered most of the main ballast pile. It was several days before the water was clear enough for us to see the entire site, but that didn't discourage the divers. What little they could see fed the flames of treasure fever. Swimming within arm's reach of $400 million can do that.

Before any work could be done on the motherlode, Hurricane Bob hit the site. Winds and seas grew and we had to pull in all the boats. Everyone returned to port to wait out the storm except the *Saba Rock*, which braved the high seas to guard the site.

On Monday, July 22, two days after the discovery, the entire company gathered for a meeting before heading back to the wrecksite. The office was a madhouse. News of the find had been picked up by the national press the day before. Now, reporters swarmed the office, each clamoring for an exclusive. Though I wanted to join in the celebration, there was a lot to do before we returned to the site. I had to get our mapping materials in order, and we had to make a 20-by-30-foot grid to lay over the site, similar to the one we used to excavate the *Margarita*. Without it, we couldn't compile a photomosaic of the hull and timbers, which were strewn over a 20-square-foot area, nor register the position of the artifacts.

At this point, the grid was the least of my worries. More critical was building a team of archaeologists to help me with the arduous task of excavating the shipwreck. I hoped that any professional archaeologist that I contacted would jump at the opportunity to work on the *Atocha*. But in my heart I knew I'd meet some resistance.

Many archaeologists shied away from shipwrecks in general. Add to that the fact they'd be working with a group of treasure divers and it amounted to professional suicide. They'd all seen what I'd been through at the professional meetings and the beating I'd taken in print. I would have a hard enough time recruiting graduate students to help develop my archaeological program. How was I going to attract experienced archaeologists and conservators who could withstand the peer pressure and cultivate a solid working relationship with Treasure Salvors' office staff and divers?

My first call was to Jim Bellis, whom I had met while working in Ghana. Jim was teaching anthropology at the University of Notre Dame, and, though we hadn't talked for several years, I still considered him a good friend. Jim was happy to hear from me, and sounded interested in the challenge. But I knew he was worried about what his colleagues would say if he worked with a commercial salvage company.

"It sounds intriguing," Jim said politely, "but, to tell you the truth, my wife and I are taking the kids on vacation in a few weeks. Besides, I just became a certified diver and I'm not sure I have enough experience underwater yet."

I understood Jim's reluctance, but I tried to reassure him that his university experience would really help in teaching the divers proper archaeological techniques.

"I need you to help me develop an operating plan," I said, trying not to sound too desperate. "I need someone to talk to, someone

Atocha Hull

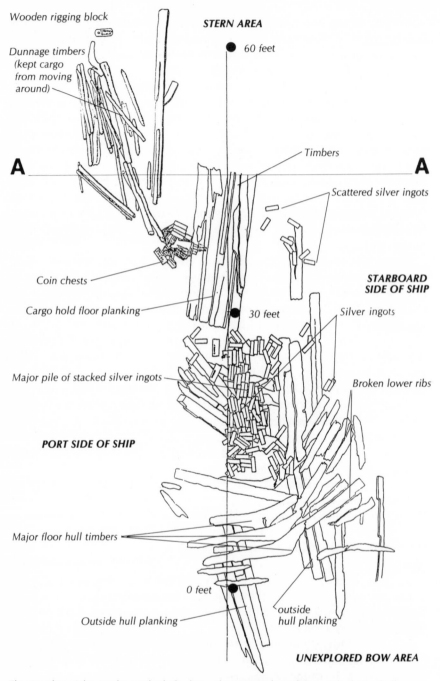

The site plan of the Atocha motherlode shows the scattered condition of the lower hull. About 30 feet of the lower hull have been uncovered to date. The hull planking and main lower frame element are in relatively good condition but clearly reflect the tremendous impact of the Atocha on the Outer Reef reported by survivors.

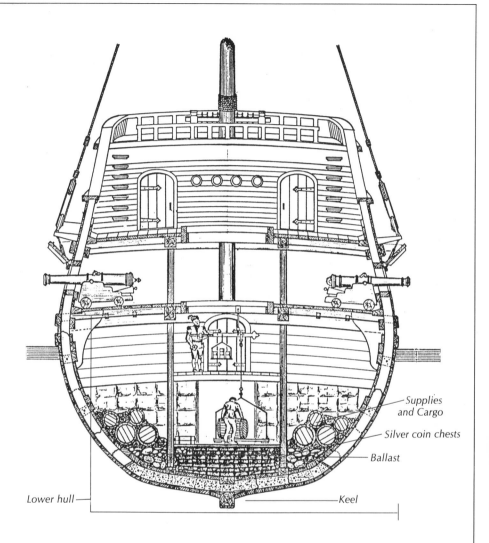

Supplies and Cargo

Silver coin chests

Ballast

Lower hull

Keel

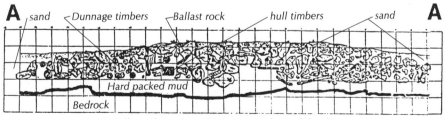

A   sand   Dunnage timbers   Ballast rock   hull timbers   sand   A

Hard packed mud

Bedrock

Ballast pile cross section across midpart of the ship

A cross section of the motherlode shows the slight mounding that was expected. While the weights of the silver ingots and ballast had pressed the wreckage into the bottom sediment, it still protrudes about three feet above the natural sea bed.

who can be my sounding board for new ideas. You really don't need to dive. Just help me organize the divers into a workable team."

"I'll think about it and let you know," Jim said.

Strike one, I thought. This may be harder than I realized. At Jim's suggestion, I called John Dorwin, an experienced diver and archaeologist from Bloomington, Indiana who had formed his own archaeological consulting company. A few years ago John, who had his doctorate in anthropology, had worked on shipwrecks off the North Carolina coast with Stephen Gluckman, a Florida anthropologist and marine archaeologist I had worked with several times. If anyone understood the archaeological signficance of this shipwreck, it was John.

I was surprised to find that John knew all about me and my work with the *Atocha*. We talked briefly about the difficulties of working with treasure hunters, and the criticism he would face from the academic community. We hit it off immediately. John didn't flinch at the challenge. He seemed to welcome being on the cutting edge of something new and innovative. "I need somebody to help me maintain good archaeological control on the site, I stressed. It is not going to be easy. We will have lots of problems at first, but I'm sure it can be done. I want you to know that if you do work with me you will be heavily criticized by some of your colleagues."

"No problem," he said. "I'll take care of that. If you want I'll come down for a few days as soon as I can get away. After that, we'll decide together whether or not there's a place for me on your team." I liked the sound of John and kept my fingers crossed that he would join the project.

News of the discovery had already reached Canada by the time I called Walter Zacharchuk, a marine archaeologist I'd met years ago at a conference. I had gotten to know Walter and his wife well during their many short vacations in Key West over the years. We had talked for hours about the work I was doing with Mel and the possibility of doing similar work with another salvage company. We also talked about the tension this type of archaeology created among our academic colleagues. I was always impressed with Walter's professionalism, and knew that we could work very well together. Six months earlier, I had invited him to join in an archaeological project on the 1715 fleet as a consultant.

Walter had extensive experience as a marine archaeologist. In the 1960s, he helped Michael Katsev and George Bass set up airlifts for their excavations in the Mediterranean. More recently, he served as the chief underwater archaeologist for Parks Canada. And though Walter never earned a degree in archaeology, he's considered by many to be one of the most eminent shipwreck archaeologists in this part of the world. I desperately needed Walter's experience in setting up airlifts and mapping the hull structure. I didn't have to ask twice. Walter would come to Key West as soon as he completed his professional obligations to Parks Canada.

Nancy Demyttenaere, a former conservator at the American Museum of Natural History in New York, was next on my list. Nancy's experience could improve our documentation process and greatly contribute to the development of our conservation laboratory. She was tantalized by the opportunity to spearhead a comprehensive conservation program, but cautious nonetheless. Nancy was worried about what her colleagues might say. She needed some time to think about the offer.

It didn't take her long to decide. A few days later, Nancy agreed to join the team. I was delighted. Nancy's laboratory experience would aid tremendously in preserving the artifacts in the water tanks. She was also a diver, which meant that she could help develop recovery procedures to ensure that the artifacts weren't damaged in handling.

I only needed one more person to complete the team—a shipbuilder. There was only one person for the job, Bill Schwicker, a local shipbuilder, sailor, and diver. As a shipbuilder, Bill viewed timbers a little differently than a ship historian such as Bill Muir, who had been with us for five years. A ship historian focuses on the design and construction of a shipwrecked vessel, comparing the broken timbers to the building contract. An archaeologist seeks to interpret the structural information in cultural terms. But a shipbuilder concentrates on the details—the grain of the wood, the weight and thickness of the timbers, and the fasteners. With Bill Schwicker's keen attention to detail, Bill Muir would be able to reconstruct the *Atocha* and provide enough historical background for me to compare the archaeological findings with the contract.

Bill immediately agreed to join the project. A few days later, I got a call from Marilyn Bellis. She, Jim, and the kids had already started for Key West. And on a recommendation from John Dorwin, a sixth person, Mike Carlson, joined the team to computerize our entire archaeological operation. The "A Team," as it came to be known, was in place, but I still had to face the initial work on the motherlode without them.

In the staff meeting on Monday, July 22, we reviewed our mapping procedures. It was important that the recovery get off to a good start. Jerry Cash and several divers had worked all night to complete the 20-by-30-foot plastic grid. Hurricane Bob was slowly moving away, and Mel wanted to get the divers back on the site.

With the weather breaking, I knew that everyone would rather be diving on the *Atocha* than listening to my speech about the historical significance of the motherlode. I couldn't tell whether I had gotten my point across, particularly to the divers who had only been with the company a short time.

Over the past few years, some divers had really gone out of

their way to help me with the archaeology. Others didn't see my side of the story; they just wanted to find treasure. I had received excellent cooperation back in 1975, but now this was a different situation. I questioned whether the newer divers sitting in front of me understood anything I had said.

"I'll be working alongside you, but I can't record all the artifacts myself." I said, stressing the importance of their role as divers *and* archaeologists. "Don't worry if things don't go well in the beginning. Each day we'll all learn how to do it better. If we learn from our mistakes and do the best job we can to record the artifacts, we'll do just fine."

"The whole world's watching us," I continued. "We've spent 16 years looking for the *Atocha*, and I don't want the whole site destroyed overnight. Other archaeologists are going to be particularly critical of our work. If you do the best job you possibly can, then, in the end, we'll have done a good job archaeologically."

That afternoon, the *Dauntless*, *Swordfish*, and *Virgilona* returned to the site and began digging on the mound. The grid was laid. But in setting the boat anchors, the grid had been pulled off the ballast pile. It lay crumbled, off to one side. If we didn't start mapping the site immediately, we'd lose a lot of critical archaeological data.

The large plastic grid wasn't working out. It was getting in everyone's way, so we needed to devise a better mapping system. There was mass confusion on the site. The ship captains seemed to be in a race, each vying to pull up treasure faster than the next guy. The whole project was out of control. Mel was in Key West negotiating with potential investors. Bleth was busy dealing with the press. Don Kincaid was shooting photos for *National Geographic*. Someone had to take charge of the operation before we destroyed the wrecksite.

That night I had a heart-to-heart talk with the crew of the *Swordfish*. "I'm not going to waste my time trying to organize good archaeological procedures if you guys aren't going to cooperate. This job cannot be done without your help. Either we develop a team to record the artifacts, or I'm going to cash it all in," I said. I had hoped they would see their responsibilities to assist me as Mel's previous divers had. All I got back were blank stares.

It seemed that now that the pile had been found, archaeology didn't matter much anymore. "We're not concerned with archaeology like you are," they quipped. "We're treasure divers. If you want to do archaeology, go off and do it the way George Bass does it. It's not fair for you to ask us to do archaeology when Mel expects us to find treasure."

The divers pointed to the name Treasure Salvors on the side of the boat. "That's our name and that's what we do. We want to find treasure. We don't want to do all the archaeology for you and then have the *Dauntless* crew find all the treasure. We're out here for the same reason they are—to find treasure, not to be archaeologists."

I repeated my speech from the Monday morning staff meeting, but it was obvious I was losing them. I had to make a move.

Early the next morning I returned to the *Dauntless* for a planning session. I solicited the crew's opinions on the best way to map the artifacts on the bottom at the same time recovery operations were underway. We decided that instead of resetting the big grid, we'd use smaller grids and lay a base line down the middle of the site. This would give us a mapping control over the entire site without getting in the way of the salvage effort. Also I wanted to number the timbers as quickly as possible so work could proceed at once to map them in position.

To the delight of the reporters and photographers who crowded around, the *Dauntless* crew continued to bring up silver ingots. Meanwhile, Mike Rizzo, Jerry Cash, and I laid the base line along the main axis of the site. Visibility was bad, and we weren't absolutely certain of the total extent of the site.

We were almost finished laying the line when Kane Fisher decided to "blow" with the mailboxes. Within seconds an enormous sand storm enveloped us as we tried to keep our balance on the bottom. I looked over and saw Jerry and Mike holding on to the ballast pile while tying down the base line and adjusting the long tape measure that paralleled the line. I couldn't believe that Kane was digging near us, especially after our discussion in the staff mettings. It was the worst thing he could be doing to this delicate mound of artifacts.

I was numb. So numb, that all I could do was sit on the bottom of the ocean in a whirldwind of sand and cry. I wept thinking of all the time and energy I'd spent getting to this point—the finding of the motherlode. I wept thinking of the promise I'd made to the press and to my professional colleagues that I was going to adhere to the highest archaeological standards.

What was going on now hardly represented the highest archaeological standards. We'd found the main hull of one of the most important Spanish shipwrecks in the Americas, and it was being blasted by the propwash of the salvage boat. The silver ingots rocked back and forth on top of the timbers as water churned around them violently. In a matter of minutes the blowers had disturbed the surface of the rock ballast and the precious silver ingots that were stacked on top of them.

Maybe my critics had been right all along. Maybe the *Swordfish* divers were right—Treasure Salvors main business is treasure hunting, not archaeology. I have devoted 12 years of my life to proving that commercial salvage and archaeology could co-exist. I had sacrificed my professional standing among my colleagues, my career, even my marriage. I felt I was watching my whole life evaporate in a cloud of sand.

I couldn't contain my anger any longer. I swam to the surface, climbed the ladder on the *Dauntless*, not even bothering to take off my gear, and stomped into the wheelhouse. It was obvious to Kane that I'd had enough.

"You don't have to like me but you have to respect me," I screamed. "I know that you're the salvage master, but I'm the archaeological director. You can't do your job and I can't do mine unless we cooperate. If you want me to continue as Treasure Salvors' archaeologist, you're going to have to cooperate."

"It's not fair to expect Jerry and Mike to work on the bottom in a sand storm. If you don't stop those blowers right now, I'm through. Your father wants to go down in history as the man who discovered the *Atocha*, not the man who destroyed it. Unless you start working with me, this whole site will be destroyed in a matter of days."

No one said a word, but Kane grabbed the throttles and quickly killed the *Dauntless'* engines. Crew members, reporters, and photographers stared, stunned into silence as I reached for the radio to call Mel at the Key West office. "I demand a meeting with you and the Board of Directors. Unless we start doing archaeology on this site, right now, I quit."

Mel was worried that the reporters would hear our conversation and he cut me off. I couldn't have cared less who was listening. Five minutes later Bleth called to say that Mel was on his way. He wanted to have a meeting on the *Dauntless*. I returned to the bottom to help Mike and Jerry finish laying the base line.

In my anger I didn't give Kane a chance to respond. We worked together on the *Margarita* site and had gotten to know one another. What I wasn't aware of was that Kane didn't even know we were down there mapping.

Things were going much better on the bottom. Jerry and Mike had made incredible progress despite all the commotion. The base line extended 150 feet through the middle of the site. They had saved the day. With the base line down, we were able to set up buoys at 30-foot intervals. We tied measuring tapes along the base line at various places to help us pinpoint the location of each artifact for our site map.

By the time we'd finished, Mel was aboard the *Dauntless*. Our discussion was tense, although Kane and I understood each other's feelings. We had already lost an awful lot of archaeological information during the first couple of days, but we could make up for the losses.

I didn't pull any punches with Mel. "I don't want to walk away from this operation after spending so many years trying to get where we are today," I said. "But I will unless you, Kane, and I work out a basic understanding. There will be no more digging with the mailboxes on the motherlode. You can dig off the mound in deeper water to look for more of the trail. But our work on the motherlode can't be disturbed with sand storms. Digging will only be done with airlifts. Two boats can work airlifts simultaneously providing we have someone

annons

As two divers watch, one of nine bronze cannons found on the Atocha site is brought aboard the salvage boat Seaker in 1976.

The Atocha carried 20 bronze cannons on her gun deck. The discovery of the cannons on the sea floor marked the scene of the breakup of the gun deck. This information proved a vital clue in locating the bulk of the galleon's treasure. After she sank, the Atocha's top decks—including the gun deck—broke off and drifted away from the main part of the hull, which contained most of the treasure. The contents of these top decks and the sterncastle were found first, starting in 1971. It took four years to find the first cannon and ten more years after that to follow the trail of the wreckage back to the motherlode.

As the encrustations were cleaned the weight markings and the four-quartered shield of the Hapsburg coat of arms became clearly visible.

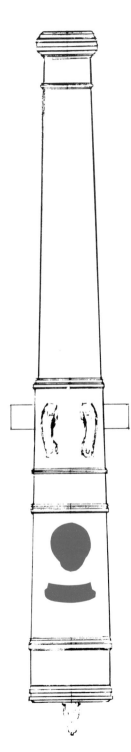

On a research trip to Seville, Gene Lyon found a list of the Atocha's bronze cannons, complete with numbers, indicating their weights. The numbers below the touchholes, on the cannons found, positively matched the numbers on the document—there was no question that these cannons belonged to the Atocha.

The ultimate weapon of the 16th century, these cannons were cast of bronze. Bronze cannons were able to withstand tremendous internal pressure, and so could be loaded with more gunpowder, hurling their 16-pound balls farther and harder than an iron cannon of comparable size. Their effect on the wooden sailing ship hulls of the era was devastating. A few shots carefully placed just below an opponent's waterline was enough to quickly sink even the largest naval vessels.

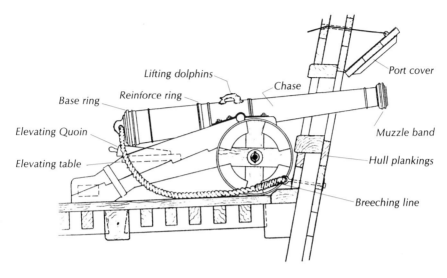

Base ring
Elevating Quoin
Elevating table
Reinforce ring
Lifting dolphins
Chase
Port cover
Muzzle band
Hull plankings
Breeching line

A reconstruction of what a mounted Atocha cannon looked like drawn by the projects' ship historian Bill Muir.

Cannons on the deck of the recovery vessel after 350 years underwater.
When each cannon was cast, its weight was marked on the barrel. Because of slight variations in the casting process, the weights were sufficiently unique to be used in place of serial numbers when listing guns on the register of arms carried aboard.

Before the cannons were moved, a photographic mosaic was made, enabling the researchers to determine the precise location and orientation of each cannon. The lay of the cannons—in two groups separated by about 30 feet, the width of the Atocha—suggested to archaeologists that the cannons fell off the deck as it rolled from side to side.

By carefully plotting the spatial relationship of each cannon as it lay on the sea floor, archaeologists determined the direction of the floating gun deck, which eventually led them to deeper waters and the motherlode.

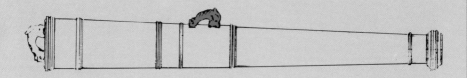

The five cannons in the first group lay exposed on hard botton, and most of the inscriptions had been worn away. The four cannons in the second group, however, were covered by a layer of fine silt, protecting them from erosion. Many of the fine details of the craftsmanship— such as on the lifting rings cast in the shape of dolphins—were still in excellent condition.

recording and mapping the artifacts as they're uncovered."

Mel knew it was important to go slow. He wanted to conduct the recovery operation professionally, just as I did. Both of us knew the whole world was watching. Mel understood the importance of doing good archaeology. Mel also had a difficult personal problem to face: Kane's boat, the *Dauntless*, wasn't equipped with airlifts. To do what I asked, he'd have to move his son, who'd found the motherlode, out of the salvage area. My concern was whether he could get his feelings across to the divers. If they believed that he was only interested in salvaging the treasure as quickly as possible, it would be difficult to get the divers to cooperate with me. Long ago I realized that doing good archaeology on the *Atocha* site meant not only understanding the historical importance of the artifacts, but keeping the lines of communication open between Mel and the divers. Mel made the right decision and stopped the use of the mailboxes.

Mel managed to tone down the feverish exuberance of the divers. His touch was magic, and over the next few days, archaeological recording procedures settled into an excellent routine. Jim Bellis and Nancy Demyttenaere the first consultants to arrive, began working with the boat crews. Tom Ford and his entire crew on the *Swordfish* began to respond to our archaeological needs. Their attitudes seemed to have changed dramatically since our discussion in the wheelhouse.

As the artifacts were uncovered, K. T. Budde-Jones measured the distance of artifacts to the base line. Her husband, Syd, compiled the site maps and drew up an intricate plan of the hull timbers and the stack of silver ingots. This time-consuming mapping enabled Paul Busch, Bill Barrons, J. J. Bettencourt, and the other divers on the *Swordfish* to record artifact positions on underwater slates as they worked on the bottom.

The more experienced divers aboard the *Virgilona* and *Dauntless*, and *J.B. Magruder* helped train the younger divers on their boats. In a matter of days, we were able to create some unity among the divers and their skills were improving rapidly. Now the boats were using nothing but airlifts and venturi pumps to dig on the mound. The frenzied activity of the first few days gave way to organization. Working together, Kane and I had been able to establish control on the site. It brought back memories of the team we'd pulled together 12 years ago. It was a good feeling.

While the divers began to record more finds, the reporters and photographers pressed them for information and photographs of the silver ingots and coin chests. It was difficult to keep the crew isolated from the media's enthusiasm and keep them focused on mapping and tagging the artifacts on the bottom before they were brought to the surface. Several times I lost my patience with some of the reporters. They were feeding the treasure fever at a time when we were trying to keep the operation under control.

National Geographic sent a film crew to shoot a television special on the motherlode. Mel had appeared on the *Tonight* show just after the motherlode was found, and had invited Johnny Carson, an enthusiastic diver, out for a look. We were all pleased and surprised when Carson's private jet landed at Key West. The press had a field day photographing Carson in his dive gear before and after the dive.

Jimmy Buffett, the singer, had long been friends with Mel and the Treasure Salvors crew. Back in Key West for a rest, he too visited the site. Buffett sat on top of silver ingots stacked up on deck and sang one of his tunes, "A Pirate Looks at 40."

These celebrities gave the media people something to talk about and photograph, and generally helped to calm the atmosphere aboard the boats. In addition to their positive effect on the crew's morale, Buffett and Carson genuinely helped the project settle down.

By the middle of August we had a better idea about the nature of the site. The treasure rested in about 53 feet of water, one foot of water shy of the estimate recorded by Gaspar de Vargas in 1622.

The main axis of the site lined up northwest to southeast, just like the artifact scatter patterns we had been following all those years. The main part of the ballast pile measured approximately 75 feet long, 30 feet wide and four feet deep at the center. Our mapping showed that the site was incredibly similar to what we had expected as described in my Masters thesis written eight years earlier.

The stern of the ship lay pointed northwestwards, with the bow pointing to the southeast towards the Outer Reef. I remembered what John Cryer, who had put our hurricane model together in 1975, had said about the storm. With the ships running without sails, the ships had turned "at cross purposes to the wind." That is they were "weather cocked," with the high poop deck which projected far above the main deck, catching the wind like a sail. This had turned the ships around so they were sailing backwards as they crossed the Outer Reef.

In the pile of timbers, we found no evidence of the keel, or keelson—the backbone of the ship. We were also missing the entire stern section, including the towering sterncastle, and the bow. We had found what remained of the sterncastle in the Quicksands, and the absence of the bow confirmed reports in the Spanish documents that the bow was battered on the Outer Reef as the *Atocha* tried to anchor. They also told us that Indians in the Keys had found part of the bow shortly after the wreck.

The evidence of the horror of the *Atocha*'s last moments was laid out on the sea bed. With her bow ripped open by the collision with the Outer Reef, the weight of the ballast and the treasure cargo in the bottom of the ship must have sunk her like a rock. It's no wonder that only 5 of the 265 passengers survived.

On November 14, 1985, Mel's daughter Taffi Quesada held a meeting to review the progress of the salvage. Her report was impressive. Within the next few months the numbers of artifacts would grow: 1041 silver ingots; more than 115 gold bars of various shapes and sizes weighing more than 250 lbs.; over 60 gold coins, most of them two-*escudo* pieces minted in Spain; 200 copper ingots; more than 30 wooden coin chests containing over 100,000 silver coins; over 750 pieces of silverware; more than 350 uncut emeralds; thousands of pottery sherds, and a whole range of objects of everyday use which will tell us much about what life was like under sail 350 years ago.

Several prominent shipwreck historians visited the site. Dr. Joe MacInnis, a Canadian researcher and early pioneer of underwater exploration came down. MacInnis had led the expedition that found the *Breadalbane,* and had worked with the group that found the *Titanic.* Also, Robert Stenuit, a world-famous archaeologist who had excavated wrecks of the 1588 Spanish Armada off the coast of Ireland, came to look at the site.

As our first season of diving on the lower hull structure came to an end, it was clear there was much more work to be done before we'd unlock all of the *Atocha's* historical mysteries. The weather was closing in on us. The winter winds that had bedeviled Gaspar de Vargas' search efforts in 1622 now began to slow us as well. We returned to the site one last time, carefully covering it with sheets of heavy-duty plastic weighed down with sand and ballast. These sheets would protect the hull timbers and archaeological deposits from being disturbed by the winter storms while we planned a second diving season.

Archaeology on Trial

Finding the hull of the *Atocha* took 16 years. Recovering the cultural wealth of the site could take even longer. The wrecks of the 1715 treasure fleet, first located in the 1960s, are still yielding valuable archaeological information and quite a bit of treasure. While Kane's dramatic discovery of the main pile ended Mel Fisher's quest, for the archaeological team this is only the first phase of a long, arduous process. I can't predict how long it will take to raise, clean, catalog, preserve, and then study and report on the 300,000 or so artifacts we eventually expect to recover from the *Atocha* and *Margarita*. Mel has won his battle with history, but for me, the archaeology of the project is still very much on trial.

When I joined Treasure Salvors on Independence Day, 1973, I wasn't just the only archaeologist working with Mel—I was the only archaeologist in the country who *would* work with a commercial salvage operation. I believed then, and still believe, that archaeologists and commercial salvors can work together on historical sites. To my professional colleagues, that's a radical notion. They believe that the interests of archaeologists and those of shipwreck salvors are diametrically and unalterably opposed.

As a result, for most of the time I've been associated with Treasure Salvors, I've been blackballed in the archaeological community. On several occasions, I was prevented from giving papers at archaeological conferences and have been discouraged from submitting reports on the *Atocha* site to professional journals.

When I joined Mel, I had three major goals: To map the site and describe the findings, to interpret the artifacts, and to tell the public and the academic community everything I could about the 1622 ships.

To map and record our finds, I worked to weld the treasure divers into an archaeological team and to train other company personnel in archaeological mapping, and curating and drawing artifacts.

In the early years, I was the only one in the company with archaeological experience. I did everything from mapping the site to cataloging the artifacts. As I trained the staff to do more of this work themselves, I was able to spend more time on the second goal—interpreting the finds.

This required more archaeological knowledge than I was able to convey to the divers as on-the-job-training. It therefore entailed tapping the specialized knowledge of other professionals. Slowly people with academic backgrounds like Claudia Linzee, Jim Sinclair, and Austin Fowles joined our in-house staff. At the same time, outside professionals from universities and museums were brought in to help improve our expertise and to make their own studies of our material. The one-person archaeological staff has now grown to a team of 15, and at present, more than 20 outside scholars are involved with the interpretation of the *Atocha* and its artifacts.

My third goal, is to educate the general public about the meaning of our finds. This has already begun. We have plans to expand the number of publications, as well as museum exhibits, a traveling display, films, and video programs already developed. A permanent museum has been built in Key West to house the core of the artifact collection. Two films have been produced for TV by *National Geographic* about the search for the *Atocha*. Millions of people all over the country will see for themselves some of the wonderous things Mel and his divers discovered. And although it will take years to fully study the vast number of artifacts, a preliminary scientific description of the site and the artifacts is scheduled for publication in 1988.

Treasure Salvors has made an enormous investment in treating, conserving, curating, and making available for study the artifacts and knowledge recovered from this site. The salaries of the professional staff, the conservation lab, and the expense of a custom-designed computer installation cost Mel—who once couldn't even afford to pay his divers—hundreds of thousands of dollars annually. Despite these expenditures and the sincere efforts of the Treasure Salvors staff and other scholars brought in as consultants, I am certain that all of us will be roundly criticized by the academic and government archaeologists. "Not precise enough," they'll say. "Not careful enough. Not slow enough. It was still a treasure hunt."

There is merit to the basic argument behind some objections. Archaeology is a destructive science. Once a site has been excavated, it can never be put back together. The contextual data, the spatial relationships that are so critical to proper interpretation of a site, are destroyed. Yet, historical sites are part of our common heritage, and the informa-

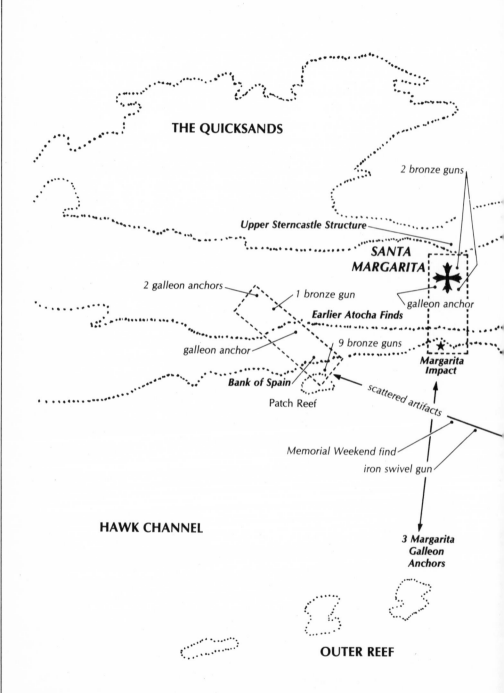

THE QUICKSANDS

2 bronze guns

Upper Sterncastle Structure

SANTA MARGARITA

2 galleon anchors

1 bronze gun

galleon anchor

Earlier Atocha Finds

9 bronze guns

galleon anchor

Margarita Impact

Bank of Spain

Patch Reef

scattered artifacts

Memorial Weekend find

iron swivel gun

3 Margarita Galleon Anchors

HAWK CHANNEL

OUTER REEF

A schematic map of the sinking and break-up of the Atocha and Margarita.

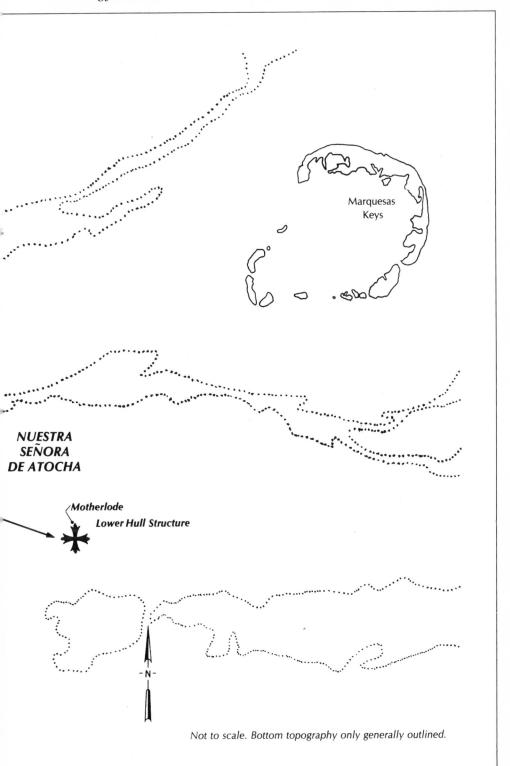

Marquesas
Keys

**NUESTRA
SEÑORA
DE ATOCHA**

Motherlode

Lower Hull Structure

- N -

Not to scale. Bottom topography only generally outlined.

tion they contain belongs to everyone. In the process of excavating a site, the archaeologist assumes a responsibility to the public to proceed carefully, extracting every morsel of data from the site as it is dis-mantled. Because so much is unknown about everyday life aboard ship, every artifact, no matter how small or seemingly insignificant, might be important. Each must be mapped as it is removed, then cleaned, preserved, studied, and curated. Treasure hunters usually can't be bothered with digging slowly, with careful mapping, or with tagging and conserving every splinter of wood, every shred of pottery. The treasure hunter is only concerned with the valuable artifacts on a site.

For these reasons, the academic archaeologists would prefer that historic shipwrecks be left on the bottom, intact, until a non-profit institution can fund their excavation. In effect, if they had their way, they would shut the doors to anyone who doesn't have an advanced degree in anthropology or archaeology. They've promoted federal legis-lation that would do just that. If the wrecks could remain safe indefi-nitely on the bottom, this approach might make sense. But they won't. As our work on the 1622 galleon shows, shallow water shipwrecks on exposed reefs and shoals are continuously deteriorating as their artifacts are shifted around on the bottom. Not only have the *Atocha* artifacts in the Quicksands been uncovered and exposed repeatedly to destruction in the ocean for over 350 years, and the *Margarita's* hull was almost certainly exposed to periodic deterioration before we found it.

I believe our work on these sites will eventually vindicate my conviction that good archaeology is possible during a commercial sal-vage effort. There certainly are pressures to work quickly, but archaeolo-gists have successfully excavated land sites for years while staying just one step ahead of the land developers and highway contractors.

We did not move as slowly as we would have in an ideal archaeological expedition, but we were not on a treasure hunt either. Treasure hunting never involves serious record keeping, and we have an extensive record of our work. But a full-blown scientific expedition, a comprehensive interdisciplinary project, was impossible on this site. Somewhere between these two extremes, I believe I developed a sound archaeological salvage program. We did the best we could under the circumstances, and a lot more than any government or academic agency would have done to find and recover the 1622 fleet. Mel said it in 1977: "We go through all kinds of hell out on that rough ocean. We're risking our lives and doing a lot of dangerous things. The state officials would not do that. The people they hire don't have the incentive, the will; they don't have that feeling for the hunt. They aren't going to be rewarded even if they do find it. To them, it's just another paycheck and I don't think they would ever succeed."

If Treasure Salvors had not found and recovered the ships, they would still be sitting down there, deteriorating. There isn't a museum in the country that has the endowment money to gamble $8 million on the *chance* of finding an historic shipwreck. Mel Fisher did.

Within recent years the Federal Government has sponsored only one historic shipwreck project—a survey of the ironclad *U.S.S. Monitor*. The State of Florida, with its Spanish heritage and thousands of important wrecks, has never paid for the excavation of a single historic vessel. If, as they claim, the state is so eager to do good ship archaeology they could map the 1715 and 1733 sites or they could locate and excavate the fleet of the French Huguenot Admiral Jean Ribault. Ribault sailed to Florida in 1564 to relieve the beleaguered French colony at Fort Caroline, on the site of what is now Jacksonville, but his flotilla was ambushed by the Spaniards. Their ships captured or burned, the French Protestant sailors were taken ashore at Matanzas Inlet and asked, one by one, to convert to the Roman Catholic faith. When they refused, each was beheaded. Their defeat effectively ended the French challenge to Spanish power in southeastern North America. It's doubtful that Ribault's ships will ever be recovered by commercial salvors, yet their excavation would add immensely to our knowledge of Florida's early history and of French seafaring technology.

The issue facing all of us is not whether commercial salvors or non-profit groups actually do the work on these sites. Our primary concern should be to preserve the eroding archaeological information. Commercial salvors are the only ones who have the money to recover these precious time capsules before they dissolve in the seawater that surrounds them.

Since my pioneering work with Treasure Salvors began, more archaeologists have gotten involved with the private salvage companies as university jobs and government grants have dried up. Now, there are more than a dozen archaeologists working as consultants for salvage companies. The trend is accelerating.

The genie is out of the bottle. Archaeologists no longer have the legal right to bar private salvage companies from working shipwrecks. The long court battles fought over the *Atocha* have crystallized a whole new body of laws dealing with historic shipwrecks, affording new options to salvors everywhere in the country. The years of haggling have left us with a much simpler set of guidelines, as defined by federal judges. First, shipwrecks more than three miles from land can be placed under federal jurisdiction and fall under the provisions of Admiralty Law and what is known as the "American Rule." The American Rule, essentially, amounts to "finders-keepers" when it comes to abandoned shipwrecks. A more recent Florida ruling stipulates that Admiralty Law has precedence over state laws even on shipwrecks within the three-mile state territorial limits. The courts have established a tradition that, if Admiralty Law is to be applied to an historic wreck, the salvor must apply acceptable archaeological controls during its recovery.

There is a danger that uncontrolled salvage and depredation by hobby divers could result in the destruction of a great number of shipwrecks. I believe the way to prevent this is through education. A former adversary has joined me in this effort. Charles M. McKinney III, an archaeologist for the U.S. Department of Interior who fought me on the *Atocha* project, has helped form The Atlantic Alliance for Maritime Heritage Conservation. This national non-profit group headquartered in Washington, D.C., brings together divers, shipwreck salvors, archaeologists, historians, and hobbyists from all over the country to work together to preserve our maritime heritage. The Alliance sponsors workshops across the country that teach recreational divers the basics of underwater archaeology and gives them respect for the historic value of shipwrecks. Prohibitions rarely work. If recreational divers want to find historic shipwrecks, they will find them. If government policy is to keep sport divers off of wrecks, when the divers find wrecks, they'll keep the locations secret and salvage them slowly and incompletely, destroying the sites in the process. In the Alliance program, they are rewarded for reporting the wrecks to professional archaeologists by being encouraged to assist in their study. The Alliance seeks to bring people into the process instead of locking them out. Para-professionals, such as sport divers with some basic training, can do valuable work on historic shipwrecks. So can commercial salvors.

Three years ago, a number of wrecks from the 1715 fleet were salvaged by commercial groups working with Treasure Salvors. Using archaeological guidelines developed on the *Atocha* site, a 12-member team worked with six different groups of salvors along a 50-mile stretch of Florida's east coast. This was the largest shipwreck project in the country. It directly involved over 75 people, including salvors, archaeologists, state officials, and graduate students. In three months, the project amassed more archaeological data and reports on these sites than state archaeologists have been able to generate in the past 20 years. This was possible largely because we were working under the jurisdiction of Federal Admiralty Law instead of under state statutes. The salvors were very helpful, because they were treated as an essential part of the project instead of being harassed by the archaeologists.

All of the shipwreck research, artifact conservation, museum exhibitions, and publications sponsored by Treasure Salvors, Inc. have been produced without a single taxpayer's dollar. The *Atocha* project vividly demonstrates that archaeologists should learn to use the profit motive to preserve the integrity of wrecksites being legally salvaged by commercial companies.

John S. Potter's *The Treasure Diver's Guide*, in 1960, laid the foundation for the treasure hunters of the following two decades. Now, the study of the 1622 sites—combining both historical and archaeological research—is laying the foundation for shipwreck salvage over the next decade. A scholarly approach to the study of the *Atocha* and *Margarita* has shown that there is no longer a place for treasure hunting in the 1980s. Concern for the cultural value of the 1622 sites turned a treasure hunt into a project with profound implications for the future of ship- wreck studies throughout the Americas.

 Nothing dies that is remembered. The salvage of the vessels of the 1622 fleet has jogged our collective memory by bringing to light the property of men and women who colonized the Americas. It is these memories that Treasure Salvors, Inc., Mel Fisher, Gene Lyon, and I have worked so long and so hard to preserve. Forget the jewels, forget the gold, forget the silver. These memories are the real treasure of the *Atocha*.

PART
III

"*The treasure of the* Atocha *and the* Margarita *now belongs to the 20th century. Archaeological and historical interpretation is providing new information about a way of life the passing of centuries has obscured. While gold and silver command great awe, the real treasure lies in the knowledge presented...*"

Janet M. Schneider
Executive Director
Queens Museum, New York

Beyond the Glitter... Secrets Revealed

he remains of the *Atocha* and *Margarita*, together with the vast amount of historical documentation gathered in the Archives of the Indies in Seville, Spain, are painting an exciting kaleidoscope of seafaring lifestyles. The study of these wrecks now involves dozens of scholars, each a specialist. While major efforts are being focused on the motherlode, deciphering details of the ship's construction, its cannon, supplies, and cargo, others continue to study the artifacts—which may eventually amount to 300,000 individual objects.

Each shipwreck is a time capsule, and the *Atocha* and *Margarita* are providing a window through which 17th century Spain and life in Spain's New World colonies can be viewed. As the historical documents are matched to the treasure cargo and personal possessions of passengers, we are beginning to see an extraordinarily rich and detailed tapestry of the treasure fleet system. Reading the documents and handling the remains from the sea bed, one can feel the pulse of the maritime trade as cargo passes from hand to hand, into the seaports of the Caribbean, and finally into the holds of the 1622 galleons. Although we can never completely reconstruct this era, these fragments can evoke a semblance of reality to which everyone can readily respond.

Perhaps the most complex artifacts assembled before the Industrial Revolution were large sailing ships. A 500- to 600-ton galleon was one of the most elaborate undertakings of the 17th century. A large ship such as the *Atocha* represents the culmination of craft traditions which stretch back into Medieval times. Innumerable crafting traditions used to build the hull, rig the masts, and furnish the interior makes these ships a marine museum of information about pre-industrial crafts and technology. The study of these artifacts as products of the work of artisans such as joiners, carvers, coopers, blacksmiths, pewter smiths, goldsmiths, silversmiths, rope makers, potters, and founders, presents an opportunity unrivalled on most historical sites on land. Ordinary objects that have not survived elsewhere, such as tools, are preserved in shipwrecks; much of this information has never been recorded before as there is infrequent mention of crafting traditions in the historical records prior to the 19th century.

Our studies are just beginning. It will be years before an exhaustive analysis of the artifacts of the 1622 galleons can be completed. Research on the more traditional objects of antiquity recovered from the 1622 galleons such as: pottery, bones, and organic material is proceeding no differently from the same type of studies land archaeologists are accustomed to. However, the study of the 1622 treasure items made of gold, silver, and precious gems is opening up many new archaeological challenges which historic site archaeologists have very rarely had to face when dealing with colonial land sites of this period. The following brief outline provides only a bare glimpse of how the study of precious metal artifacts recovered from the *Atocha* and the *Margarita* wrecksites are opening up new windows of opportunity for scholars to examine the pomp and power of the socially elite Spanish American colonies only a century after Columbus discovered them. The rich flavor of the archaeological potential of gold and silver artifacts from the 1622 galleons has yet to be fully tasted.

The Archaeology of Treasure

When Cortez conquered the Aztecs of Mexico in 1520, he plundered their stores of precious metals, dramatically expanding the world's supply of hard currency. Because this expanded supply was controlled entirely by the Spanish, it increased Spain's power enormously. Throughout the 16th century, the conquistadores were conjurors; they found more and more wealth to plunder. At first, they simply stole the precious goods of the natives, melted them down, and shipped them home. Soon enough they began to mine silver, gold, emeralds, and diamonds using Indian slave labor. In 1545, an Indian discovered the most famous mine, the mountain of silver at Potosi, in Peru. To keep count of the treasure more easily the Crown established mints in the colonies. The mints made bars and coins of standard value for export and, as the colonial population grew, supplied hard cash to use in New World cities.

The gold and silver bullion and coins recovered from the *Atocha* and the *Margarita* are helping historians unravel the history of Spain in the New World. The primary ways of using treasure to aid historical research are by deciphering the markings on the silver and gold, and by delving into the cargo manifests, matching the bars or coins recovered to the merchants and passengers who shipped the goods.

One of Treasure Salvors' archaeological divers, K.T. Budde-Jones, studied the markings on the gold bullion recovered from the *Margarita*. In a short time, she was able to make some headway in decoding the cryptic markings on the bars helping us to learn more about them and how they might have ended up on board.

The gold bars range in size from six to 77 troy ounces. They often carry a mark which is probably a foundry stamp indicating where they were cast; the bars also have a seal showing that the royal tax was paid; a gouge where the assayer took a bit of metal to test its purity; a karat stamp, indicating the purity; and sometimes numbers telling the weight of the bar.

Jones' work on the foundry marks shows that the bars recovered so far come from nine different foundries. The majority are stamped with the name *Sargosa* or "NAN P3" foundries believed to have been in Colombia. Each foundry produced bars or a typical size, weight, and purity. The *Sargosa* bars ranged in size from 2.3 to 2.8 centimeters wide, 23.9 to 26.8 centimeters long, and weigh an average of 29 troy ounces. The NAN P3 bars range from 2.9 to 3.3 centimeters wide and 20.2 to 28.1 centimeters long. There seem to be two basic sizes, 37 troy ounces and 71 troy ounces. Three of the *Sargosa* bars appear to have been cut. They may have been cut to their present size and weight from larger bars in order to fill a purchase order.

The *Sargosa* bars were not cast as carefully as those from other areas. The ends are often misformed, and not gently tapered or rounded. These deformities help us identify bars that aren't marked with a foundry stamp. The poor casting could have been due to the need to fill an order very quickly or it could show that a new mint had been established or an old one relocated, affecting the quality of the workmanship.

The karat stamps show the purity of the gold in Roman Numerals. A 20-karat bar would be stamped XX. The purity was measured down to the quarter karat, and these were indicated by placing a dot after or above the Roman numerals. A 21½ karat bar would be marked XXI, for example. The karat value and design of the karat stamp vary from foundry to foundry. The quarter-karat dots of the *Sargosa* bars are dots inside of a circle, while the quarter-karat stamps of the NAN P3 bars are dots enclosed in a square or rectangle. These slight differences also help distinguish unmarked bars, and can help correlate the bars to the lading documents completed in the various ports along the route of the 1622 galleons.

The nine foundries represented in the *Margarita* cargo processed gold of different purities. The *Sargosa* bars are all 20 or 22½

rtifacts

Divers use their fingers to gently push aside sand and other sediments that cover the artifacts scattered on the sea floor.

Many artifacts, especially metal ones, are often coated with a heavy marine encrustation. Proper cleaning of artifacts is not only important for restoration, but provides crucial archaeological information.

This beautiful hand-carved ivory box top was found with its silver hasp still intact. The box and half its top must have disintegrated long ago in the salt water. The design and style of the carving suggests that the box was crafted in Ceylon, and shipped out of Gao on the coast of India.

*Wealthy Spaniards who migrated to the New World brought many personal silver posses-
sions with them. This silver stirrup, unrecognizable before it was cleaned, is an excellent example of the superb craftsmanship of the silversmiths of the period. The study of silver artifacts recovered from shipwrecks can provide new information about the skills and
technology of the craftsmen and artists history books tell us very little about.*

These fragments are probably remains of a Meso-American gourd shaped bowl or container shipped to Spain on board the Atocha.

Ceramics are often used by archaeologists to provide a date for historical sites. Because decorative styles change frequently, the design of pottery can often be tied to a fairly narrow period of time. Ceramics turned up in the Quicksands area included a number of fragments of majolica, bearing the distinctive blue-on-white or white-on-blue design. By comparing the design of these fragments to those of known dates found on land sites, the Quicksands wreckage dates between 1615 and 1630. The later identification of the wreck as the Atocha reconfirmed the dating of ceramics made earlier by land archaeologists.

This lead seal marked a particular shipment bound for Spain. The raised coat of arms is that of the City of Amsterdam in Holland.

Many fine brass mortar and pestle sets have been found on the 1622 site. New World copper mined extensively in Cuba, may have helped make up the brass used to cast these vessels.

Lead seal

Mortar and Pestle

karats, while the NAN P3 bars range from 15 to 21 karats. It may be that the difference in purity reflects the quality of gold available to the foundries in different locations.

The tax seals are circular inscriptions giving the name of the reigning king of Spain, and the recipient of the *quinto*. The *quinto* was the 20 percent tax due the Royal Treasurey on all bullion shipped from the New World to Spain. The penalty for not paying the royal tax was severe, so the bars were stamped many times to ensure that a tax stamp would be visible even if the bar was cut into smaller sections to pay for purchases. The seals were affixed by hammering a die into the surface of the bar. The seals rarely went on evenly, and no examples of complete seals have yet been recovered from the *Atocha* or *Margarita*.

The assayer's bite, a small scoop of metal taken to test purity, was normally taken from the tip or side of the bar. The assayer who tested the *Sargosa* bars occasionally took his sample from the top of the bar. This deviation could indicate that someone was filling in for the assayer at the times those bars were tested. Some bars lack the assayer's bite. It appears that, if a number of bars were poured from one batch of gold, only one bar might be tested. Or, it's possible that some gold might have been poured off for testing before the bars were cast.

In the summer of 1982, 16 gold bars that showed no assayer's bite, tax stamps, or foundry marks were found on the *Atocha* site. These bars were smaller than the other bars, and averaged 22 troy ounces in weight. The only marks on these bars were the karat stamps and the number showing the weight in *pesos de oro*, the Spanish weight measurement. The bars were found close to the emerald cross and a religious ring which probably belonged to an important church official. These bars may have been consigned to the Catholic church, and thus exempt from the king's tax. This may be the reason for the superior quality of the casting. It's also possible that this gold was being smuggled back to Spain under the protection of the church's tax exemption.

Coins

Much of the treasure carried by galleons was in the form of eight reale coins, more popularly known as "pieces-of-eight," Silver was also minted in denominations of four, two, one, and one-half reales.

Silver coins, unlike gold, are affected by salt water. When recovered, silver coins are usually covered by a thick crust of corrosion and, sometimes, coral or other marine accretions. The coins may be fused together in a big mass called a conglomerate. The coins have to be cleaned electrolytically. After the surface encrustations are removed the coins can be weighed, photographed, and studied.

Numismatists—coin historians and collectors—have long been fascinated with the silver and gold coins recovered from sunken treasure galleons of the 16th and 17th centuries. Although numismatists have studied large assemblages of coins from shipwrecks, archaeologists have not. Spanish American coinage closely reflected coining methods devised by Italian Renaissance artists such as Leonardo da Vinci and Benvenuto Cellini early in the 16th century. The method used in the New World mints was simple. First, silver was drawn out into a rod the same diameter as the finished coin. Planchets, or blanks, of the appropriate thickness were then clipped off the end of the bar. The coins were then struck by hand with an engraved die and a hammer. The resulting coins were called "cobs," an English corruption of the Spanish *Cabo de Barra*—literally "cut from a bar." In many cases cob coins were struck off center, leaving much of the die design missing.

Coins provide archaeologists with one of the best tools for dating shipwrecks. While most coins minted before 1732 don't bear a specific date they do carry the Royal coat of arms of the Spanish king in power at the time the coin was minted. Thus they can be dated within a definite period.

Numismatic historians use the characteristics of dies to establish relative dates of coins within a particular king's reign. Each successive die used during a king's reign is unique in some small way. One of the ways to distinguish dies is through the flaws, such as cracks, irregularities in the wording, and engraving errors. Other dies differ stylistically in details such as variations in parts of the Hapsburg shield.

Thus, linking the use of certain distinctive dies to the dates coins were struck with can then help establish a date for shipwrecks. The relative dates for various dies can be inferred from the combination of unique obverse (front) and reverse (rear) dies used on a particular coin. The reverse die was the punch die and took the full brunt of the blow from the hammer. The reverse die wore out much sooner than the obverse die, which was placed in the anvil; the obverse die was protected from direct hammer blows and usually outlasted the reverse die which were normally not as well engraved.

Under normal circumstances it was not unusual for a single obverse die to last as long as three reverse dies. Three coins, each struck with the same obverse die could have been struck with three different reverse dies. Also, two coins struck with the same reverse die could have been struck with different reverse dies. In the same way land archaeologists build sequences of pottery designs to help them date land sites, sequences of coin dies can help build a chronology for coins from a particular mint.

The study of the silver coins from the *Atocha's* motherlode is helping to rewrite the early numismatic history of the New World. As over 100,000 coins are cleaned and studied within these individual coin chests an enormous amount of contextual data never before recovered from a shipwreck will be computerized for analysis by scholars all over the world. This study is being undertaken with close cooperation from the American Numismatic Association.

Gold Coins

The wealth of gold coins recovered from 17th and 18th century shipwrecks has helped fill in large gaps in the history of Spanish American coins. In particular, the discovery of the galleons of the 1715 fleet off the Florida coast brought to light some of the rarest and historically important gold coins from several different mints. These coins were minted during the last ten years of the reign of Charles II (1665–1700), the last Hapsburg King, and for 15 years during the reign of Philip V (1700–1724), of the House of Bourbon. Since the early 1960s, when large numbers of cob coins began to be found on these wrecks, numismatists and collectors have marvelled at the exquisite detail and beauty of gold coins minted at Lima and Cuzco in Peru, Bogota in Colombia, and in Mexico City.

Gold coins were struck in denominations of one, two, four, and eight *escudos*. The eight-*escudo* piece, also called "onza" or "doubloon," usually weighed about 27 grams, or .87 troy ounces.

Although Spanish gold coins of the 19th century have been available to collectors for years, gold coins from the 17th and 18th centuries are still very scarce. Gold coins weren't regularly minted in the New World until the Mexico City mint began striking them in 1679. One numismatic authority estimates that, on average, each Royal mint produced about 4000 gold coins annually during the 25 years between 1690 and 1715. Probably no more than 400,000 gold coins of all denominations were minted prior to the sinking of the 1715 fleet. Most of these coins were shipped back to Spain and only remained in circulation a short time until they were melted down and re-minted in the Old World.

Besides the loss of large numbers of gold coins on the 1715 fleet, large shipments were lost in other years when treasure galleons sank, such as when the *San Jose* was sunk by the English off Colombia in 1708. The loss of such large numbers of coins makes them relatively rare.

Gold coins from the Bogota mint recovered from the 1715 sites are among the rarest issued in the New World. Many of these coins weren't believed to exist before the discovery of the 1715 shipwrecks. The collections of the Smithsonian Institution and the American Numismatic Society together contained no more than ten gold coins from the Bogota mint. Despite the coins found on the 1715 fleet, gold coins from the Bogota mint are still very rare.

No gold coins were listed on the manifest of either the 1622 galleons. But two, one-*escudos* and 65 two-*escudos* were found on the north end of the *Atocha's* motherlode. These coins spilled out of the sterncastle as the personal effects of the wealthy passengers were tossed about as the upper super structure broke up.

Armor and Weapons

Men continued to wear armor well into the 18th century, even though the use of firearms had made it an anachronism. Following the American Revolution, body armor disappeared until it underwent a small revival during the Civil War. Armor made a comeback during World War I, with the issue of the steel helmet, and later during World War II with the development of lightweight materials able to stop a modern bullet that could be fashioned into flak jackets and bulletproof vests.

As the treasure galleons carried regular companies of infantry in addition to military passengers, they should yield a wealth of body armor. A metal head piece found on the *Atocha* site is probably the type of helmet known as an "archer's salade." These were open-faced, close-fitting helmets, widely used in Northern Europe. These usually had a broad "tail" which covered the back of the wearer's neck. Later versions of these helmets were frequently made in two pieces which fastened around the base of the headpiece. Several helmets similar to the one found on the *Atocha* were excavated some years ago near Santa Fe, New Mexico. These were believed to have been made between 1490 and 1510 and left behind during Juan de Onate's expedition into New Mexico in 1597 and 1598.

Documents and contemporary drawings give a good picture of the armor of the conquistadores. A number of pieces have survived on land sites, giving scholars an idea of how early explorers such as Coronado and de Soto adapted European armor to their long treks across the American continent. Shipwrecks, because they can be definitely dated, can give more exact information about the types of armor that were used at specific times in history.

Body armor from shipwrecks is never easy to identify. The metal corrodes quickly in salt water and attracts coral and other kinds of encrustation. Body armor has probably gone unrecognized on a number of Spanish shipwrecks off Florida because divers have lacked experience in identifying encrusted pieces. When the helmet was recovered on the *Atocha* site, Treasure Salvors divers and state archaeological agents thought it was either a bomb fragment from the nearby Navy bombing range or something that fell off a modern boat. The longer I looked at the shape and the small rivet holes running around the base, the more I was convinced it was a two-piece helmet from the *Atocha*. Once the encrustation had been removed, it was easily recognized as something far more than just modern rubbish. Another time, two small encrusted objects which had been put aside by divers were recognized as spurs by photographer Don Kincaid. Kincaid's experience in handling many artifacts, gained over the last 20 years, has given him an uncanny knack for recognizing objects through thick encrustations. These two incidents prove the first rule of shipwreck archaeology: everything must be recovered from a site and nothing should be discarded until it has been closely examined by someone experienced in interpreting artifacts.

Metal Working

Following the Dark Ages, the artistic traditions suppressed during the early Christian era flowered again in Italy during the 15th century. This was the Renaissance, and it spread gradually to France, then to England and other parts of Europe. Nowhere is this rekindling of the western world's artistic spirit better represented archaeologically than on Spanish treasure wrecks of the era. The splendid gold and silver objects found on Plate Fleet vessels are a documentary on the rebirth of metal working during the early Renaissance.

In the 15th and 16th centuries, silver dinnerware graced the tables of the affluent once again. Since then, the art of silversmithing has been gauged by the quality of the dinnerware popular at any given time. The silver dinnerware found on early shipwrecks in the Americas was made by some of the finest European craftsmen of the time. Much of it reflects the crafting tradition associated with Benvenuto Cellini (1500–1571). Cellini, a contemporary of Michelangelo, became world-famous as one of the leading Renaissance artists.

Spaniards delighted in an ostentatious display of wealth. This was apparent through the way in which clothing and weapons were decorated, and also in the use of silver and gold objects for everyday purposes. The history of Spanish colonial silver dates from the beginning of colonization of the Caribbean Basin since the time of Columbus. As wealthy Spaniards migrated to the New World, they brought many silver personal possessions. Silversmithing began almost immediately: Licensed silversmiths had come to the New World before 1516.

Probably no craft is as rich in tradition as silversmithing. Regardless of technological innovations, delicate silver objects can only be made by master craftsmen. While silversmithing today is faster, using newer manufacturing processes, silversmiths still must be highly trained. This experience can't be learned overnight; the craft is handed down slowly over a period of time by a master craftsman to his apprentices. The study of silver objects from shipwrecks can provide new information about the skills and technology of the people who made them. Only a small percentage of silver dinnerware has survived on land, making the silverware of shipwrecks doubly important. Ware from

A huge amount of ship's hardware has been found on the 1622 galleons. Thick, heavy iron objects, such as this lock (above), the iron rigging hook, the lead sounding weight and the boat hook (below, right to left) were able to withstand many centuries of immersion in the corrosive seawater. These simply-made objects tell us about life under sail centuries ago.

Leg irons or shackles can be readily identified even when heavily encrusted. The irons were used to restrain slaves or even crewmembers. On board a ship thousands of miles from the nearest civilian or military court, strict discipline was necessary. An unruly crew could easily overpower the small number of officers, and while dangerous, piracy was far more lucrative than being a common sailor.

Silver Pitcher

These silver ewers or pitchers recovered from the Atocha show how native American silver-smiths integrated their traditional design motifs into European-styled objects. This intermingling of styles can also be seen in objects created by Spanish craftsmen in Europe which reflect the influence of Meso-American design.

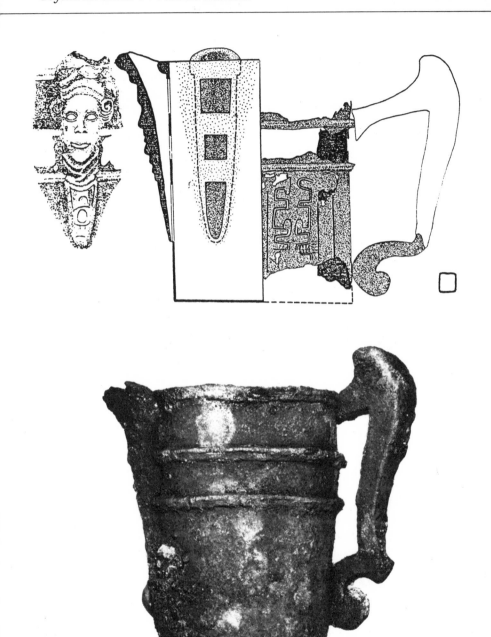

the workshops that produced it may be rare even in large European museums. Though we may not know the name of the workshop or the master who ran it, we can study the level of craftsmanship and its ornamental style. The style of decoration can help indicate where and when an object was made.

Spanish colonial silver was more original in its design than the more conservative pieces made in the mother country. A striking difference between pieces from Spain and those from its colonies was weight. The silversmiths of Spain hammered their objects as thin as possible. A colonial silversmith, living near a rich silver mine, might use three or four times as much silver of the same object.

The styles of each colony varied, so that workmanship from Peru is noticeably different from that of Mexico. Objects made in the cities by master craftsmen are more delicate and sophisticated than those made in the provinces by blacksmiths, serving as silversmiths.

The richly-decorated churches of Mexico and Central and South America reflects the relative splendor of ecclesiastical silver throughout the New World colonies. By Church law, chalices and patens to hold the bread and wine of the Eucharist had to be made of precious metal and their interiors lined with gold. The Society of Jesus, founded in Spain in 1534 by Ignatius Loyola, was one of the most active both in the Empire's fight against the Protestant Reformation and in missionary work in the New World. One means used by the Jesuits to promote Catholicism was to proclaim the wealth and power of the Roman church through an ornate style of art, now known as Baroque. This became the orthodox style of church ornaments everywhere in the Spanish Empire, although some local variations exist. The chain of rural missions established in Paraguay in 1610 is noted for its distinctive decorative architectural style. Metal objects made by the area's Indians under Spanish direction reflects a blending of elaborate European motifs with native interpretations. Unfortunately, when the Jesuits were expelled from all Spanish dominions in 1767, the missions were abandoned and their silver objects were scattered. Many of the decorative pieces were melted down to be reshaped into more modern forms, and few survived. The pieces on the 1622 galleons, are prime examples of the type of religious artifacts that today are very rare. As hundreds of pieces of rare and beautiful silver altarware of all shapes and sizes are carefully cleaned, preserved, and studied, the splendor of the *Atocha's* motherlode becomes more apparent than ever.

Jewelry

The universal fascination of jewels comes not only from their beauty, but also their ability to express a wide range of human emotions such as love, superstition, religious devotion, and political allegiance. Jewelry is more than a work of art; it's a unique testimony to human aspirations. The many jewels recovered from shipwrecks of the 16th and 17th centuries provide a glimpse into the lifestyles of the period and the inventiveness of artists and craftsmen.

Although extensive documentation exists in both written and pictorial form, nothing verifies the role of the artist-craftsman as well as the many beautiful gold objects recovered from Spanish shipwrecks pre-dating 1750. Jewelers' designs, materials, and techniques of the 16th and 17th centuries reflect the final vestiges of Medieval art, as well as the humanistic and classical ideas of Renaissance art which played such a major role in shaping Western thought.

Spaniards quickly realized that some of the richest gold deposits in the New World were in the icy mountain rivers of western and central Colombia. By the 16th century, plentiful supplies of gold flowed from the mountains to the seaport of Cartagena, where it was loaded on to treasure ships bound for Spain.

Goldworking flourished with the Indian societies of Central and South America for many centuries before Spanish discovery of the New World. Unfortunately, few examples of this workmanship has been preserved, as the conquistadores melted down nearly every Indian gold object they could obtain and shipped it back to Spain as gold bullion. As a result, most of the Pre-Colombian Meso-American gold and silver objects displayed in museums today were recovered from graves and therefore have very little research value.

Indian goldsmiths were the elite in the socially developed regions of Mexico, Colombia, and the Peruvian highlands. Spaniards marvelled at the Indians' highly-refined goldworking skills and their ability to produce high-quality filigree goldware using the lost-wax process.

During the 16th and 17th centuries, one of the safest ways to preserve private wealth was to turn gold and silver into jewelry. As a result, gold and silversmiths in Spain and her American colonies were much in demand. At the peak of Spain's hegemony over the Caribbean basin, much of her wealth of precious metal was evident in the treasures of the elite.

Renaissance jewelry was more than just a tangible reflection of personal vanities; jewels were a major thread of the social fabric, commerce, and marriage dowries, and the wealth of ruling monarchs.

The vast quantities of gold and precious stones found in the New World stimulated a rebirth in jewelry design throughout Europe. The decorative art influence during the Renaissance carries over to jewelry and goldsmithing. The Renaissance was truly the age of elaborate jewels. The need of aristocrats to demonstrate their wealth and power created a great demand for jewelry, and therefore increased production. During the 1500s, gold necklaces and chains of every size and shape were worn by both men and women. Men were often more sumptuously dressed than their female counterparts, often sacrificing balance and good taste to their display of wealth and power. In the 1540s, Henry VIII certainly wore more jewels than any of his six wives.

Jewelry styles of the Renaissance gradually evolved into the Baroque style at the turn of the 16th century. Craftsmen found new ways to cut precious stones while, at the same time, floral designs were becoming more fashionable. There was a considerable decrease in the number of pieces worn, and it became less fashionable for men to adorn themselves with jewelry. The improved cutting techniques made diamonds the most sought-after gem. During the second half of the century, precious personal ornaments were dominated by faceted gems, as it was more difficult to mount uncut stones. The use of decorative enamel and gold declined. Numerous gems, accented by branches, leaves, and flower petals made of enamel and gold, became the principal elements of many designs. Gems were set into pendants, rings, necklaces, bracelets, and belts.

In addition to diamonds, coral was a popular gem of the 1600s. It had already enjoyed a long and distinguished history among other ancient cultures. Many believed that coral, which was exported from India, China, and the Mediterranean and Red Seas, possessed magical powers.

The 18th century was a period of great evolution and development in jewelry. Necklaces of the period were composed almost exclusively of gems of various sizes, shapes, and colors—emeralds, rubies, diamonds, and topazes. Pearls and other precious stones, though still important design elements, were less popular. They were used more sparingly and with stricter symmetry and greater discipline. Jewelry recovered from the *Atocha* and *Margarita* are helping to shed new insight about how archaeologists can use gold artifacts to learn about the social history of Hispanic America that potsherds can't tell us.

Religious Artifacts

The importance of religion in 17th century Spain can't be overstated. Catholicism permeated every aspect of Spanish culture including seafarers, who feared the wrath of God more than dying at sea.

For this reason, most Spanish galleons sailed with at least one priest, who in addition to signifying the presence of God, conducted religious ceremonies. The first light of dawn brought the entire crew to the main deck for mass. All who were not manning the vessel were expected to attend. For the wealthy passengers confronted with the vagaries of the sea, this daily ritual provided courage and comfort.

It wasn't uncommon for all passengers—whether a young sailor or a wealthy banker—to carry some reliquary as a symbol of their commitment to Catholicism and God. Many reliquaries were made of rock crystal enclosing a miniature replica of Christ, the Madonna, or the Pieta. Rosaries were a common relic and qualify as some of the most stunning pieces of jewelry recovered from Spanish shipwrecks. This is certainly true of the red coral rosary found on the *Atocha* by John (B.J.) Lewis. Fifty-three red coral beads and five gold beads accentuate the 1 ¼-inch gold crucifix. The rosary measures 11 ⅝-inches in length.

The most popular religious item was the cross, as it was the main symbol of the Christian faith. The cross was considered a powerful talisman which would bring good fortune to the faithful. Many different types of crosses made of varying materials have been recovered from shipwrecks. Gold crosses studded with gems and hanging pearls were popular during the 17th century. Religious artifacts from the 1622 wreck sites are providing tangible links to a rich part of the cultural heritage of the Americas not normally encountered on land sites.

Rings

Perhaps at no other time have rings been worn in such numbers and made to such high standards as in the 16th century. Many rings were associated with love and marriage. Some had twin hoops bearing inscriptions expressing fidelity and matrimony. Others bore the symbol of two right hands clasped together. The devout wore rings bearing emblems of faith; the superstitious wore rings as talismans. Popes, kings, and bishops donned rings as a sign of their authority. To display their wealth the elite wore rings on all fingers, including the thumb, or on chains that were draped on hats and around the neck and waist. In the 1600s, as fashion trends became more conservative, fewer rings were worn, and the designs were simplified.

A good representative sample of different types of rings have been recovered from both 1622 treasure galleons. Their comparative study will provide more clues about different facets of life centuries ago.

Pendants

At the peak of Spain's hegemony in the Caribbean, a large volume of precious metals were transformed into baubles for the wealthy. Perhaps no other object found on the wrecksites illustrates the interplay of gold, gems and enamel and superb craftsmanship as well as pendants. These intricately detailed ornaments were worn by women on chains hung around the neck and shoulders, or pinned to the sleeve.

It's difficult for historians to pinpoint the origin of most secular jewelry, as metalsmiths traveled from one country to another. Many of the figurative pendants displayed in museums throughout the world were crafted in south Germany, the hub of jewelry designers and metal craftsmen.

Many pendants were designed to serve a particular function. Pomanders were scented balls of musk or ambergris placed in containers to alleviate the unpleasant smells aboard a ship. Passengers wore earrings and neck chains made of beads and ambergris to make their journey more pleasant. Several pendants from the *Atocha* and *Margarita* are providing new insight to artistic designs popular during this period.

Accessories

Whistles were first used on English vessels in the 14th century. By the 16th century they became common on most ships. These whistles were made of gold and worn as a badge of rank by senior officers of the Spanish fleet system. Silver whistles often belonged to junior officers.

At sea, where a shouted order may not have been heard above the roar of the ocean and wind, these whistles were used to communicate a variety of commands. Crewmen were trained to respond immediately to orders for hoisting sails conveyed by different notes and pitches. The most well-known call was used for "piping the side," a signal of respect for senior ships' officers visiting other ships at sea.

By the 19th century, the boatswain (bosun) became the officer in charge of rigging sails and handling deck equipment. Because he was required to issue orders more frequently than senior officers, his whistle became known as the bosun's whistle. A bosun's whistle was recovered from the *Atocha* and the *Margarita*. Attached to a long gold chain, these whistles were worn draped around the neck on a number of strands, and may have belonged to the ship's pilot or a high-ranking official.

Although more sophisticated communication systems exist on modern naval ships, the whistle has become a nautical tradition.

Other accessories included tooth and ear picks. Toothpicks, which came in many shapes and forms, were worn around the neck or from the wrist. These objects were fashionable among the wealthy until aromatic wood picks came into vogue.

Epilogue

The site of the *Atocha*'s motherlode was "put to bed" with heavy plastic sheets for the winter in late September 1985. While Treasure Salvors suspended diving operations on the lower hull structure until the arrival of milder spring weather, the archaeological team assessed the results of the initial recovery program.

We shot hundreds of hours of videotape and began indexing the tapes and correlating them to the site plan. Jim Sinclair and his conservation staff continued to chemically treat hundreds of artifacts. The conservators made latex molds of several of the 30 wooden coin chests. The archaeological team continued the study of the hull structure from the measurements and photographs taken on the site.

We also began the task of matching the huge volume of notes, underwater site drawings, logs, and photographs with the artifacts and the conservation records generated in the lab. After each artifact was cleaned and measured, it was sketched by one of the artists working under Jerry Cash's direction. Photographs were taken of the most significant artifacts.

All of this information, so critical to the later interpretation of the site, has to be linked together to give us a complete picture of each recovered artifact: its original position on the site, the objects found near it, the boat that recovered it, its condition on entering the lab, and the steps taken to conserve it.

Two decades ago, we would have most likely sorted all of this information by hand. It would have taken many months just to properly catalog the material before the analysis of the site could begin. However, under the direction of Mike and Mark Carlson, Treasure Salvors purchased and installed some $250,000 worth of computer hardware for the sole purpose of cataloging the finds. As we continue to analyze the site, we'll be able to quickly cross reference the artifacts in the assemblage in a variety of ways. This installation is the first time a computer has been used to catalog and interpret so much material from an historic shipwreck.

With these resources, the *Atocha* and *Margarita* sites are providing a tremendous amount of new archaeological information about the Spanish Colonial Americas.Much of this information is difficult to obtain from land sites. Relatively few Spanish Colonial land sites have been scientifically examined, and those that have been excavated have yielded few artifacts. Over the years, almost a quarter of a million artifacts have been recovered from the *Atocha* and *Margarita*. Aside from the silver, gold, and jewels, the collection includes an enormous amount of pottery and other utilitarian items vital to the study of past lifestyles.

Not only have the 1622 galleons provided a vast and varied assemblage of artifacts, but the shipwrecks themselves provide a definitive date for this collection. It's often difficult to precisely date individual artifacts from land sites because there may be several superimposed layers of material, each from a different time period. In the case of the *Atocha* and *Margarita* material, we know that all of the artifacts were being used together when the galleons sank on September 6, 1622.

Finally, the *Atocha* and *Margarita* have provided one more critical link: historical documentation. Gene Lyon's excellent historical research has produced more specific information about these sites than is possible on land sites of this period. We not only know a great deal about the ships and their contents, we also know something about the people, the crew and passengers. We know their names and for some, even their personal histories.

This is the real purpose of archaeology: to enable scholars to reconstruct the fine detail of history and increase our understanding of life in the past. Gene Lyon's research provided the archaeological detectives with important clues to the location of the 1622 galleons. Now, with the ships in hand, we are able to furnish historians with a vast new body of raw material that will help them better understand the European exploitation of the Americas.

rchaeological Techniques

Clusters of artifacts on a site can indicate the part of the vessel that is being excavated. Their pattern on the bottom can also reveal the sequence of events that led up to and followed the sinking. In the case of the Atocha, the failure to find the main hull in the immediate vicinity of the anchor made this kind of interpretation a practical necessity.

An aerial view of a salvage boat digging with mailboxes in the Southeast Corridor taken from 6,000 feet up shows a cluster of dark spots indicating areas that have already been excavated.

Mel Fisher's "mailbox," invented for his salvage efforts on the 1715 fleet, revolutionized underwater salvage techniques. Deflectors, fitted over a boat's propellers, channel the boat's prop wash to the bottom, thereby blowing aside loose sand concealing artifacts.

Magnetometer runs are coordinated by observers in a tower. Using theodolites—a combination range-finder, direction finder, and telescope—two or more operators radio the boat captain towing the magnetometer to keep him on course as the sensor is pulled through the water. (Right) Here a diver helps position one of the deflectors or "mailboxes".

Divers use a small airlift (top) to carefully excavate around the fragile remnants of the Atocha's wooden hull. The mailboxes on the sterns of the salvage boats generate too much thrust for this delicate work, so the timbers are uncovered by hand. These wooden hull fragments are among the rarest artifacts found on the 1622 site—only a few galleon hulls have been recovered worldwide. (Below) The techniques for excavating, mapping, and studying the Atocha's hull were pioneered during Treasure Salvors' recovery of the hull of the Margarita in 1980.

The Margarita's hull section was 23 feet long. All of the timbers were carefully lettered and numbered, and a photomosaic was made of the entire site.

Pat Clyne and Mel Fisher *prepare the camera track used to create the photomosaic (overleaf) composed of 130 separate photos of the* Margarita's *hull.*

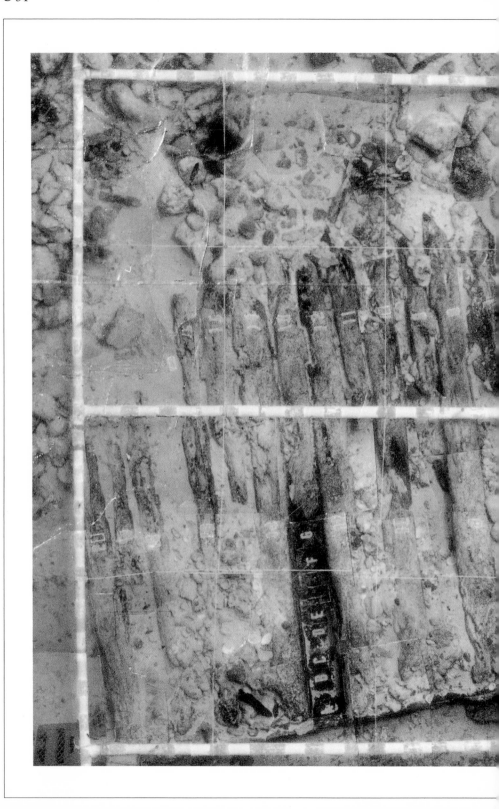

The Margarita hull timbers must have been covered by sand, protecting them from the wood-eating teredo worms. Also, the ballast was clean, free of barnacles and other growth, suggesting that the whole site had been buried. A PVC mapping grid was laid over the timbers and a baseline established through the middle. This allowed the timbers to be measured very precisely for accurate drawings and studies.

Study of the ribs and outside planking (strakes) have helped clarify certain passages in the construction contract of the Atocha. These articulated timbers are providing details about a number of unique architectural features including scarf joints, fastening procedures, and framing techniques. Plans are being considered to recover and chemically treat the hull structure so it can be exhibited in a major museum display.

Syd Jones maps the Atocha motherlode site piece by piece. Precise underwater mapping is critical to a successful archaeological dig. The spatial relationship between the artifacts on the site can give investigators crucial clues.

A grid was constructed of plastic PVC pipe. The grid, marked off in one-meter sections, was used to measure the distance between artifacts on the sea floor. Divers recorded the location of artifacts, not only in terms of their distance from two edges of the grid, but also noting the amount of sand that covered them.

Galleon anchors can be up to 16 feet long and weigh more than a ton. Divers measure the heavily-encrusted anchor of the Atocha, which was found on the site in 1971. The anchor was left on the bottom as a reference point until 1978, when it was no longer needed for bottom mapping. After its recovery, several well-preserved inscriptions were found under the encrustation.

Here Don Kincaid shows museum visitors how he found one of the ten anchors that have been recovered from the wrecks of the two Spanish galleons. These anchors provide valuable insight into the events leading up to the impact, sinking, and disintegration of both ships.

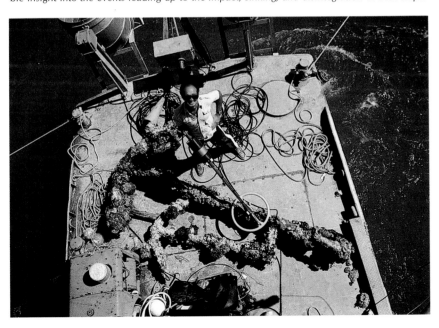

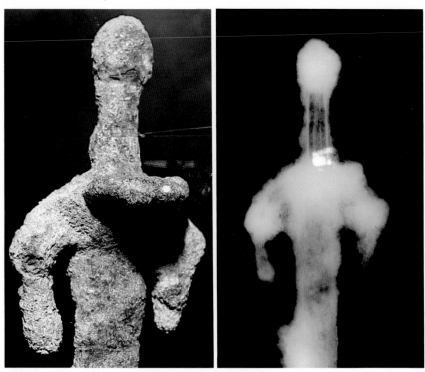

Three centuries under water left the swords found on the Atocha heavily encrusted. Although the details couldn't be seen, some were obviously rapiers, displaying the common wide, sweeping hilts. X-rays were taken of 26 sword hilts. The x-rays revealed the design of the rapiers, in most cases. This helped to positively date the wrecksite. Here however, the x-ray shows that there was not enough metal of the sword remaining to attempt restoration.

This unusual find is a piece of pottery fully intact recovered from the motherlode site by Bill Barron.

Silver coins, unlike gold, are affected by salt water. When recovered, silver coins are usually covered by a thick crust of corrosion, coral, or other marine accretions or the coins may be fused together in a big mass called a conglomerate. The coins are then cleaned electrolytically. After the surface encrustations are removed the coins can be weighed, photographed, and studied.

Kane Fisher, captain of the Dauntless discusses the next move with Greg Wareham (foreground)and Andy Matroci, the divers who found the motherlode.

There is very little difference between archaeology underwater and on land. The same basic tools and procedures are used. Archaeologists used this underwater plane table and transit to compile maps of the Atocha wrecksite. The Atocha project demonstrated conclusively that shallow-water shipwrecks in the Americas can be recovered with the same strict controls used by dry-land archaeologists.

The careful measurements and precise photographs helped archaeologists reconstruct the path of the Atocha as it drifted and broke up, eventually leading searchers to the "mother lode."

A small camera tower attached to a measurement grid was used to record one-square yard areas. This makes a photographic record of important finds situated on the bottom.

Proper archaeological procedures are followed on land as well as mapping the site on the sea floor: All of the artifacts recovered are carefully cleaned, catalogued, drawn, and photographed. The research team includes (clockwise from above) Dr. Gene Lyon, D. Larissa Dillin, Leah Miguel, Else Pederson, (below left to right) Bill Schwicker, Bill Muir, Walter Zacharchuk, David Moore, and Jerry Cash.

Archaeological puzzles come in all sizes. Here Duncan Mathewson closely examines a piece of a book found on the Margarita site.

Mel Fisher was the leading force in the search for the treasure of the 1622 galleons. His struggle to find the lost treasure has been a costly one, both financially, and personally. But the search continues, this mound of silver bars and coins are a small portion of what has been found. Excavation of the motherlode site is expected to continue for several years.

Appendices

1. *Treasure Salvors Inc.*

2. *Selected Bibliography*

1

Treasure Salvors Inc.

It is impossible to list all the people who have been involved with *Treasure Salvors, Inc.* over the last 16 years. A number of boat captains and divers who were instrumental in first locating and mapping the **Atocha** remains in the Quicksands area are no longer with the Company. Many people have come and gone over the intervening years. Digging boat captains: Ian Koblich of the **Golden Venture**; Earl Mundt of the **E-Z Living**; John Brandon of the **Endeavor**. Search boat captions: Bob Moran; Bob Holloway; Ray Dozier; Denny Breese; and Arnold McLean. Archaeological conservators: Claudia Linzee Pennington; Austin Fowles; and Rick Murphy. Divers: Kay Finley Holloway; John "B.J." Lewis; Scott Hammond; Tim Marsh; Warren Hough; Roger McLean; Steve Wickens; Hugh Spinney, Jim Solanick; Joe Spangler; and Mike Schnaedelbach are only a few who have made major contributions leading up to the discovery of the main part of the wreck. Their team effort is not forgotten by those people listed below who were there when the lower hull structure was located on July 20, 1985 and those who continue to search off the Marquesas Keys.

Board of Directors

President	Mel Fisher
Secretary/Treasurer	Dolores E. Fisher
Vice Presidents	Don Kincaid
	Eugene Lyon, Ph.D.
	Jud Chalmers

Public Affairs

Vice President	Bleth McHaley
Secretary	Chloe Schroder

Administrative Staff

Executive Secretary	Judy Sojourner
Secretarial Assistant	Chris Elwonger
Bookkeeper	Sandy Dunn
Receptionist	Kathryn Simpson

Research and Development

Sea Search Consultant	Fay Feild

Operational Staff

Logistics Operations Mgr.	Ted Miguel
Videographer	Patrick Clyne
Assistant Photographer	Damien Lin

M/V Swordfish

Captain	Tom Ford
Archaeological Mappers	Syd Jones
	K.T. Budde-Jones
Crew	Bill Barron
	J.J. Bettencourt
	Ralph Budd
	Michael Burns
	Paul Busch
	Toni Marsh
	Michael More
	Pat Willoughby
	Julie Fisher

M/V Bookmaker

Captain	Kim Fisher
Archaeological Mapper	Chip Clemmons
Crew	Stephen T. Williams

M/V J. B. Magruder

Captain	Donnie Jonas
Archaeological Mapper	Dick Klaudt
Crew	Giacomo Amoroso
	Don Deeks
	Pedro Estrada
	David Jonas
	James McNair
	Tom Roberts
	Vincent G. Trotta III

M/V Dauntless

Captain	Kane Fisher
Archaeological Mapper	Andy Matroci
Crew	Thomas Barham
	Frank Lutz
	Bill Moore
	Del Scruggs
	Chuck Sotzin
	Steve Swindell
	Greg Wareham

M/V Virgilona

Captain	R. D. LeClair
Archaeological Mapper	Spencer Wickens
Crew	Randy Barnhouse
	Kim Dickson
	Edgar H. Hinkle
	Mike Mayer
	Scott Nierling
	Bill Reighard
	Curtis White

M/V Saba Rock

Captains	Don Durant, Jr.
	Ed Stevans
Archaeological Mapper	Susan Nelson
Crew	Jim Featherson
	Librado Manzueta
	Sterling Rivers
	Jeff Voss

M/V: Motorized Vessels

Exhibition and Gift Shop

Manager	Jose Quesada
Personnel	Caroline Brinkley
	Sherry Culpepper
	Grace Fisher
	Terry Fisher
	Catherine Medeiros
	Anita Parker
	Sonia Smith
	Tom Barham
	James Skelton

Archival Research

Historian	Eugene Lyon, Ph.D.

Curating Department

Director	Taffi Fisher Quesada
Personnel	Linda Halvorson
	Leah Miguel
	Brent Moody
	Else Pedersen
	Scott Pinto
	Alisha Sabul

Cartography Department

Senior Cartograher	Ed Little
Ass't. Cartographer	Steve Taylor

Conservation Department

Conservator	James J. Sinclair
Lab Technicians	Frederick Ingerson
	Tony Kopp
	Sean McKinney
	Bruce Stephenson

Art Department

Director	Jerry Cash
Draftsmen	D. Larissa Dillin
	Kathleen Garvin
	Rollin McGrail

Archaeological Department

Director	R. Duncan Mathewson III, MA
Archaeologists	John T. Dorwin, Ph.D.
	David D. Moore
	Walter Zacharchuk
Lab Technicians	Mike Riccio
	Jim Vonderhaar
Ship Historians	Bill Muir
	Bill Schwicker

Computer Department

Director	Michael L. Carlson
	Mark A. Carlson

Legal and Accounting Department

Attorneys	David Paul Horan
	Rick Bannon
	William Vandercreek
	Joshua M. Morse III
Accountant	Rose Chibbaro

Research Consultants

Over the years, a number of scholars from the academic community and museums have participated as private consultants in the study of the 1622 material. The following researchers have made major contributions. Institutional affiliation is given only for identification purpose:

James O. Bellis, Ph.D.
Dept. of Anthropology
Notre Dame University
South Bend, IN

Andrew A. Benson, Ph.D.
Scripps Institution of Oceanography
San Diego, CA

Dale Billman,
Resource Analysts, Inc.
Bloomington, IN

Nancy Demyttenaere, MA
Archaeological Conservators,
New York State Parks,
Recreation and Historic Preservation,
Bureau of Historic Sites
Albany, NY

Derek J. de Solla Price, Ph.D.
History of Science
Yale University
New Haven, CT

Harold E. Edgerton, Ph.D.
Department of Engineering
Mass. Institute of Technology
Cambridge, MA

Col. Robert H. Green
Associate Editor
Silver Magazine
Key West, FL

Stephen Hale, Ph.D.
Anthropology Department
University of Florida
Gainesville, FL

John F. Hayward, D. Litt.
Art Historian
Sotheby, Parke, Bernet
London, UNITED KINGDOM

Gary E. Kozak
Sales Engineer
Klein Associates, Inc.
Salem, NH

Robert W. Luce, Ph.D.
SCS Engineers, Inc.
Reston, VA

Joseph B. MacInnis, MD
Underwater Research, Ltd.
Toronto, CANADA

Michael Marcial
Emeralds International, Inc.
Key West, FL

James H. Mathewson, Ph.D.
Department of Oceanography
University of California
at San Diego
San Diego, CA

R. F. McAllister, Ph.D.
Department of Ocean Engineering
Florida Atlantic University
Boca Raton, FL

Sandy McKinney
Numismatist
Key West, FL

Priscilla E. Muller, Ph.D.
Museum Curator
Hispanic Society of America
New York, NY

Lee Newsom
Anthropology Department
University of Florida
Gainesville, FL

Curtis E. Peterson, MA
Conservation Department
Institute of Archaeology and
Anthropology
University of South Carolina
Columbia, SC

Robert B. Pickering, Ph.D.
Physical Anthropologist
Field Museum of Natural History
Chicago, IL

Barbara Purdy, Ph.D.
Anthropology Department
University of Florida
Gainesville, FL

Janet Schneider, MA
Executive Director
The Queens Museum
Flushing, NY

Eugene Shinn, Ph.D.
U.S. Geological Survey
Virginia Key
Miami, FL.

Portia Takakjian
Ship Historian
Piermont, NY

Henry B. Taylor III
American Numismatic Association
Islamorada, FL

Joseph Ternbach, Ph.D.
Conservator
Queens, NY

Jim Thomas, MA
Marine Biologist
Ramrod Key, FL

Harold R. Wanless, Ph.D.
Department of Geology
Rosentiel School of Marine and
Atmospheric Science
University of Miami
Miami, FL

Jack Zbar
Chemist
Arrow Engineering, Inc.
Dalton, GA

Graduate Students

Since 1973, a number of university students have participated in the on-going archaeological work on the 1622 sites and in the laboratory. The following student assistants have played a major role in the research effort while working for their degrees:

Kathleen M. Bernard, BA
Anthropology Department
Notre Dame University

Patrick Kilbride, BA
Marine Studies Department
University of the Virgin Islands
St. Thomas, Virgin Islands

Jan Fisher, BA
History of Ideas
Williams College

Mitchell W. Marken, M. Litt.
Institute of Maritime Studies
University of St. Andrews
Scotland, UNITED KINGDOM

Christen M. Gober, BA
Anthropology Department
Indiana University

Keith A. McIntyre, MA
Anthropology Department
University of Florida

Steve Hamburg, MA
Anthropology Department
Florida Atlantic University

Rick Trembley, BA
History Department
Florida International University

Thomas H. Ingram, MA
Anthropology Department
Florida Atlantic University

2

Selected Bibliography

I *Major Publications*

Burgess, Robert F. *They Found Treasure*. New York: Dodd, Mead & Co., 1977. pp. 15–75, 170–238.

Daley, Robert. *Treasure*. Random House, 1977.

Dranov, Paula. "Hi-tech Treasure Hunt." *Science Digest*, Vol. 90, No. 12 (December 1982): pp. 60–65.

Lyon, Eugene. "The Trouble with Treasure." *National Geographic Magazine*, Vol. 149, No. 6 (June 1976): pp. 787–809.

——. *The Search for the Atocha*. New York: Harper & Row Publishers, Inc. First printing, 1979. Florida Classics Library, second printing, 1985.

——. "Treasure from the Ghost Galleon." *National Geographic Magazine*, Vol. 161, No. 1 (February 1982): pp. 228–243.

Mathewson, R. Duncan, III. "Method and Theory in New World Historic Wreck Archaeology: Hypothesis Testing on the Site of *Nuestra Señora de Atocha*, Marquesas Keys, Florida." MA Thesis, Florida Atlantic University, Boca Raton, Florida (1977).

——."Archaeological Treasure: The Search for the *Nuestra Señora de Atocha*." Seafarers Heritage Library, 1983. Second printing 1985.

Schneider, Janet M., Susan T. Lubowsky and R. Duncan Mathewson III. "Shipwrecked 1622, The Lost Treasure of Philip IV." Catalog for Queens Museum. 1981.

Treasure Salvors, Inc. "Spanish Fleet, The 1622 Treasure of the *Nuestra Señora de Atocha* and *Santa Margarita*." Catalog, 1980.

——. "The Treasure of 1622." Catalog, 1981.

Wade, Nicholas. "Galleons Yield Gold, Silver, and Archaeology." *Science*, Vol. 212, No. 4502 (June 1981): pp. 1486–87.

II *Manuscripts and Conference Papers*

Lyon, Eugene. *1622 Fleet Loss Narrative.* ms. (n.d.a.).

_____.*List of Gear and Equipment and Some Construction Details of Nuestra Señora de Atocha, 1622.* ms. (n.d.b.).

_____. *Data on the Identification of Shipwreck Site 8M0141 in the Marquesas Keys, Florida.* ms. (1975).

_____. "The Identification of a 17th-century Spanish Galleon, *Nuestra Señora de Atocha.*" Paper presented at the St. Augustine Historical Society (1976).

_____. "Spanish Cultures in Colonial Florida and Their Connection with Historic Shipwrecks." Paper presented at the Conference on Florida Historic Shipwreck Archaeology (1977).

_____. "A Historian's Thoughts on Some Shipwreck Models." Paper presented at the Conference on Maritime Cultural Heritage of the Florida Keys; How Can It Be Preserved? Florida Endowment for the Humanities, Key West, Florida (1980).

Lyon, Eugene and R. Duncan Mathewson III. "The Historical and Archaeological Meaning of the 1622 Shipwrecks Off the Marquesas Keys, Florida." Paper presented at the Florida Historical Society Conference, Gainesville, Florida (1975).

_____. "An Introduction to the Ethnohistory of the Lower Florida Keys." Paper presented at the American Society for Ethnohistory Conference, Gainesville, Florida (1975).

Lyon, Eugene and Barbara Purdy. "Contraband in Spanish Colonial Ships." *Itinerario: Journal of the Institute of European Expansion,* University of Leiden (1982).

Mathewson, R. Duncan, III. "Historical Shipwreck Archaeology: New Developments from the Lower Florida Keys." The Conference on Historic Site Archaeology Papers 1973, Vol. 8, University of South Carolina (1975): pp. 121–128.

_____. "A New Methodological Approach to Shipwreck Archaeology." Paper presented at the Society for Historical Archaeology and International Conference on Underwater Archaeology, Charleston, South Carolina (1975).

_____. "Historical Shipwreck Ceramics: A Preliminary Analysis of Olive Jar Data from the Wreck Site of *Nuestra Señora de Atocha.*" ms., Department of Anthropology, Florida Atlantic University, Boca Raton, Florida (1975).

_____. "Archaeological Recovery: Its Potential and Limitations on New World Shallow Water Sites." ms. (1975).

_____. "Introductory Notes on Operationalizing a Procedural Model for the Conservation of Archaeological Data From the Wreck Site of *Nuestra Señora de Atocha.*" ms. (1976).

_____. "An Introduction to the Numismatic Assemblage From the *Nuestra Señora de Atocha.*" ms. (1976).

_____. "Archaeological Research on the Wreck Site of the *Nuestra Señora de Atocha*: A General Overview of the Mapping and Survey Procedures." Paper presented at the Society for Historical Archaeology and International Conference on Underwater Archaeology, Ottawa, Canada (1977).

_____. "An Introduction to the Use of Aerial Photographic Imagery for Locating and Interpreting Shallow Water Shipwreck Sites Off the Florida Coast." ms., Department of Geography, Florida Atlantic University, Boca Raton, Florida (1977).

Mathewson, R. Duncan, III, and P. Clyne. "Digging Procedures Utilized in the Search for the Lower Hull Section of the *Nuestra Señora de Atocha*." Paper presented at the Society for Historical Archaeology and International Conference on Underwater Archaeology, Ottawa, Canada (1977).

Mathewson, R. Duncan III, John T. Dorwin, James J. Sinclair, and Mitchell W. Marken "*Atocha* Archaeology: A Look at the Anatomy of a Spanish Treasure Galleon." Paper presented at the Society for Historical Archaeology and Conferences on Underwater Archaeology, Sacramento, California (1986).

Mathewson, R. Duncan, III, and Eugene Lyon. "The Guns of the *Nuestra Señora de Atocha*." ms. (1976).

Mathewson, R. Duncan, III, Eugene Lyon and R. F. McAllister. "*Atocha* Data Evaluation Report." ms. (1976).

Mathewson, R. Duncan, III, Larry Murphy and Bill Spencer. "New Concepts in Marine Archaeology: Shallow Water Historic Archaeology in the Lower Florida Keys." Conference on Historic Site Archaeology Papers, Vol. 9, University of South Carolina (1975): pp. 141–151.

III   *Special Publications*

Mel Fisher Maritime Heritage Society. *Astrolabe*. Quarterly newsletter. Vol. 1–

Treasure Salvors. *The Treasure of 1622*. Museum booklet. (1981).

——. *Treasure Talk*. Quarterly newsletter. Vol. 1. (1984).

——. *Shipwreck Salvage: Exploring the Myth*. (1985).

IV   *Films*

National Geographic, Television Film Special, Educational Division. *Treasure*. (1976).

——. Explorers Television Productions. *Quest for the Atocha*. (1986).

Treasure Salvors. *Treasure Trove of the Century*. (1966).

——. *Treasure Salvors of the Florida Keys*. (1968).

V *Major Exhibitions*

Cape Coral, Florida (June 1975).

Palm Beach, Florida (September 1975).

Hilton Head, Georgia (January 1976).

Atlanta, Georgia (March 1976).

Washington, D.C., Explorers Hall, National Geographic Society (June 1976).

Miami, Florida, Omni International Hotel (December 1976).

Toronto, Canada, Harbour Front (June 1979).

San Diego, California (January 1981).

Washington, D.C., Explorers Hall, National Geographic Society, "Shipwrecked 1622." (July 22–September 13 1981).

New York, NY, The Queens Museum, "Shipwrecked 1622: The Lost Treasure of the Spanish Kings Comes to Queens." (October 17–November 29 1981).

Jacksonville, Florida, The Jacksonville Museum of Arts and Sciences, "The Sunken Treasure of the Spanish Fleet, 1622." (December–January 1982).

Key West, Florida, East Martello Museum, "The Lost Treasure of the Golden Galleons." (February 6–March 7 1982).

Baltimore, Maryland, U.S. Customs House Call Room, "The Lost Treasure of the Golden Galleons." (May 1–July 11 1982).

Key West, Florida, Mallory Square Convention Center, "The Lost Treasure of the Golden Galleons." (October 22, 1982–January 16, 1983).

VI. *Permanent Exhibitions In Key West Florida*

The Golden Doubloon Galleon: *The Pirate Treasure Ship and Museum of Sunken Treasure.* (1971–1978).

The Lost Treasure of the Golden Galleons. (1978–present).

Index *

A

Accessories, recovery of, in salvage operations, 142
Admiralty Law, 90-92, 121
  and the American Rule, 121
Aerial photography, use of, in salvage operations, 85-87
Airlifts, use of, in salvage operations, 112,
American Rule, 121
Anchors
  finding of, 36, 66-67
  types carried on Spanish ships, **38-39**
Araya, 23
Arbutus, use of, in salvage operations, 80
Archaeological record keeping, use of, in salvage operations, 65-66
Archaeological techniques, role of, in salvage operations, 44-51, **52-53**, 103-105, 108-115, 116-117, 120-123
Artifact map. *See Mapping*
Artifacts, recovery of, in salvage operations, 91-92, 93-96, 102, 126-133, **134-137**, 138-142
Armor, recovery of, in salvage operations, 132-133
Assayer's bite, 129
Astrolabe, recovery of, in salvage operations, 69, **83**
A Team, 109
Atlantic Alliance for Maritime Heritage Conservation, 122
Atocha, Neustra Señora de
  archaeological evidence in search for, 10-11, 44-51, **52-53**, 70-73, 74-75, 76-79
  and the deep water theory, 64-69, 71, 78
  early salvage attempts, 25-27, **28-29**, 30
  finding of the motherlode, 97-99, 102-105, **106-107**, 108-115
  manifest documents of, 34, 62, 71, 92-93
  protection of remains, 143-144
  reconstruction of, **20-21**, 95
  recovery of artifacts from, 50-51, **52-53**, 54-55, 58-59. 62-63, 98-99
  search for, 14, 31-37, 40-41, 88-96
  sinking of, 17, 18, 23-24, 59, 62

B

Bañon, Juan, 27
Barrons, Bill, 113
Bass, George, 108, 110
Beede, Kevin, 85
Bellis, Jim, 105, 108, 109, 113
Bellis, Marilyn, 109
Berrier, John, 37, 89, 96
Bettencourt, J. J., 113
Boca Grande Channel, 36
Bookmaker, use of, in salvage operations, 98
Brandon, John, 66, 78
Breadalbane, 115
Brunton compass, use of, in salvage operations, 67-68
Budde-Jones, K. T., 99, 113, 128
Buffett, Jimmy, 114
Bullion, recovery of, 127-129
Busch, Paul, 113

C

Cadereita, Marquis of, 23, 25, 26, 33, 34
Cadiz, 22
Caicos Islands, 27
Candeleria, Nuestra Señora de, 23

Candlestick, as artifact, **102**
Cannons, salvage of, **74-75**, 76
Cardona, Captain Nicholas de, 26-27, 59, 63, 64
Carlson, Mark, 144
Carlson, Mike, 109, 144
Carson, Johnny, 114
Cartagena, 19, 23
Cash, Jerry, 12, 95, 109, 111-112, 143
Cellini, Benvenuto, 133
Clausen, Carl, 37, 40, 48, 68
Clemmons, Chip, 98
Clyne, Pat, 12, 70, 76, 78, 85, 93
Cockrell, William A. (Sonny), 40
Coins, recovery of, in salvage operations, 58-59, 114, 127, 129-132
Computer, use of, in documenting archaeological finds, 144
Concepcion, Nuestra Señora de la, 33
Consolacion, Nuestra Señora de la, 24
Continental Exploration, 33, 46, 89
Contrastacion, Casa de, 19, 30, 32
Copper diving bell, use of, in salvage operations, 27, 32
Coral Plateau, 67
Coronado, Juan, 132
Cortez, Hernando, 127
Cousteau, Jacques, 94
Cryer, John, 71, 114
Curaçao, 27

D

Dauntless, and the search for the *Atocha*, 14, 98, 99, 102, 104, 110-111, 112, 113
Deep water theory, 64-69, 78, 98
Del Norte navigation systems, and salvage efforts, 84-85
de Anuez, Captain Juan, 27
de Cardona, Captain Nicholas, 26-27
de Lugo, Captain Bernardino, 24, 32, 35, 62, 89
de Mineya, Lázaro Fañez, **82**
Demyttenaere, Nancy, 109, 113
de Oñate, Juan, 132
de Soto, Hernando, 132
de Ubilla, Don Juan Esteban, 32
de Vargas, Gaspar, 25-27, 59, 63, 69, 113-115
Dillin, Larissa, D., 12
Dividers, as artifact, **82**
Dominica, 22
Dorian, Alan W., 40
Dorwin, John, 108, 109
Dry Tortugas, 35, 59

E

Eastman Kodak, photographic systems of, 85
Edgerton, Dr. Harold (Doc), 81, 84
Emeralds, finding of, from *Atocha*, 98-99

F

Feild, Fay, 12, 31-32, 84
Ferreira, Alonso, **21**
Finley, Kay, 36
Firearms, recovery of, from shipwrecks, 55, 93
Fisher, Angel, 14, 73, 76-78, 80, 104
Fisher, Deo, (Dolores), 34
Fisher, Dirk, 14, 40, 71, 73, 76, 77-78, 80, **83**, 88, 97, 104
Fisher, Kane, 12, 14, 49-50, 92-93, 96, 97-98, 99, 102, 103-104, 111-113, 116

Fisher, Kim, 12, 49, 78
Fisher, Mel, 10, 14-15, 31-37, 40-41, 44-51, 62-
    63, 69, 80-81, 88-89, 90-92, 98-99, 103, 110,
    112-113, 113, 116, 121, 123
Fisher, Taffi Quesada, 12, 115
Fisher, Terry, 12
Flores, Señora Angeles, 34, 35, 36
Florida, legal involvement in salvage rights,
    32, 37, 40-41, 90-91, 121
Flux-gate magnetometer, use of, in salvage
    operations, 31,32 *See also* Magnetometer
Ford, Tom, 92, 99, 110, 111, 113
Forte, Melissa, 85, 89-90
Fort Jefferson National Monument, 35, 59
Fowles, Austin, 95, 117

                                G

Gage, Rick, 14, 77, 80, 104
Gates, Rupert, 31
Gewin, Judge Walter P., 15
Gluckman, Stephen, 108
Gold bars. *See* Bullion
Gold coins. *See* Coins
Golden Doubloon, use of, in salvage
    operations, 50
Grappling hooks, use of, in salvage
    operations, 26, **28-29**
Grenada, 30
Guadeloupe, 27

                                H

Haiti, 27
Hardware, **134-135**
Haskins, Jack, 33, 37, 46, 89, 96
Havana, 19, 22, 23, 25, 26
Hawk Channel, exploration of, 66, 67, 72-73,
    79, 80-81, 84-87, 88, 97, 98, 99, 102
Herrera, 72
Heyn, Piet, 27
Hispaniola, 27
Holloway, Bob, 36
Holly's Folly, use of, in salvage operations, 36
Holzman, Walt, 31
Horan, David Paul, 78, 92
Hydra-Flow, use of, in salvage operations,
    80-81

                                I

Indias, Carrera de, 18
Indies, Archive of, 33-34
Indies, Council of, 27
Inkwells, **102**

                                J

James Bay, use of, in salvage operations, 88
Jewelry, recovery of, from shipwrecks, 98-99,
    138-142
Jonas, Donny, 77
Jones, Syd, 84, 92, 94, 99, 113
Jordan, Bobby, 89, 91-92

                                K

Katsev, Michael, 108
Key Largo, 32, 33
Key West, 32, 35
Kincaid, Don, 12, 36, 41, 70, 72, 76, 77, 85,
    89-90, 91, 92, 94, 96, 99, 110, 132-133
Kirwin, Peggy, 85

                                L

LeClair, R. D., 91

Lewis, (Bouncy), John, 49, 78
Linzee, Claudia, 95, 117
Little, Ed, 12, 85, 89-90, 99
Littlehales, Bates, 78
Littlehales, Nikki, 78
Little Torch Key, 92
Loggerhead Key, 25-26, 35, 59, 62, 69
Lopez, Bartolome, 25, 32, 33, 69
Loran (LOng RAnge Navigation) C
    technology, and salvage efforts, 84
Lower Antilles, 27
Lower Matecumbe Key, 35
Loyola, Ignatius, 138
Lyon, Dr. Eugene (Gene), 10, 12, 34-37, 41,
    43, 44-45, 49-50, 62, 77, 78, 88-89, 93,
    95, 103, 123, 144

                                M

MacAllaster, Richard, 37, 46, 89
MacInnis, Dr. Joe, 115
Magnetometer, use of, in salvage operations,
    36, 80, 81, 84, 85, 96, 99
Magruder, J.B., 113
Mailbox, use of, in salvage attempts, 32, 49-
    50, 67-68, 72, 111, 113
Majolica, recovery of, from shipwrecks, 58
Manila fleet, 19
Mapping, use of, in salvage operations, 64-
    69, 84-85, 89-90, **118-119**
Maracaibo, Venezuela, 30
Marathon (Key), 33
March, Tim, 78
Matchlock musket, 55, **56**
Margues, Cayo de, 26
Marquesas Keys, 35
Marquez, Cayos del, 34-35
Martinique, 27
Marx, Bob, 35, 40
Matecumbe, Cayos de, 34
Matecumbe Key, 25, 32, 33
Mathewson, Duncan, III, 12, 44-51, 70-79, 92,
    97, 98, 99, 102-105, 108-115, 116-117, 120-
    123
Mathewson, Marie, 44, 79
Matroci, Andy, 102, 104
McAllister, Ray, 71, 94
McHaley, Bleth, 12, 40-41, 46, 49, 50, 73, 102-
    103, 110
McKee, Art, 31, 33
McKinney, Charles III, 122
Melián, Franciso Nuñez, 27, 32, 63, 64, **82,**
    92-93
Metal work, recovery of, in salvage
    operations, 133, **134-137,** 138
Meylach, Marty, 85
Miguel, Leah, 12
Miguel, Ted, 84, 103
Molinar, Demosthenes, "Mo-mo," (Moe), 31,
    77
Moran, Bob, 72, 97
Morgan, Captain Henry, 30
Mortar and pestle, recovery of, in salvage
    operations, **100**
Mud Deep, 67, 71-72, 80
Muir, Bill, 12, **21, 74,** 95-96, 109

                                N

National Aeronautics and Space
    Administration photographic systems of,
    85
National Geographic, 114, 117

Navigation instruments, **82-83**
Nelson, Susan, 98-99
Northwind, use of, in salvage operations, 14, 71-72, 76, 77, 78, 79, 104
Numismatic History of Mexico (Pradeau), 59
Numismatists, and recovery of coins from shipwrecks, 129-131

O

Olive jars, recovery of, in salvage operations, 58, **60-61,** 63
Outer Reef, 67, 97, **106,** 114

P

Panama City, 30
Park Bernet Galleries (New York), 32
Patch Reef, 67, 69, 70
Pegasus, 94
Pendants, recovery of, in salvage operations, 141-142
Personal possessions, **100-101**
Peterson, Curt, 95
Philip IV, King of Spain, 18, 22
Photomosaic, use of, in salvage operations, 76, 93-94
"Pirate Looks at 40, A," 114
Plus Ultra, use of, in salvage operations, 97
Portobello, 19, 22, 23, 30
Port Royal, 45
Potter, John S., Jr., 31, 32, 122
Pottery, recovery of, in salvage operations, 58, **60-61**
Pradeau, Alberto, 59

Q

Quicksands area, search for *Atocha* in, 66-67, 69, 72, 76, 88, 89, 98, 102

R

Rapier design, 55, **57**
Real, 8, 31, 72
Rebikoff, Dmitri, 94
Religious artifacts, recovery of, in salvage operations, 140-141
Ribault, Jean, 121
Rings, recovery of, in salvage operations, 141
Rizzo, Mike, 111-112
Rosario
  salvage and burning of, 25-26, 59, 62, 69
  sinking of, 59, 62
Rudder, salvage of pintles, 62-63

S

Saba Rock, 98, 99, 105
St. Maarten, 27
Salvage methods
  early methods, 26, 27, **28-29**
  technology used for, 31-32, 36, 49-50, 64-69, 72, 76, 80, 81, 84-87, 93-94, 96, 99, 111, 112
San Angustias, 63
Sand Key, 35
Sand shaker, **102**
San Jose, 131
San Juan, 94
Santa Catalina, 25
Santa Margarita, 11
  cargo manifest of, 34
  salvage of, 26-27, 34, 64, 102, 105
  search for, 25, 32-33, 36, 71, 89, 94-96, 97
  sinking of, 17, 18, 24, 35-36, 59, 62
Schneider, Janet M., 125

Schwicker, Bill, 109
Search for the Atocha, The (Lyon), 35
Search grid, use of, in salvage operations, 65, 67-68 *See also* Mapping
Sears, Dr. William H., 79
Sebastian Inlet, 31
Selanick, Jim, 77
Shipwrecks, use of coins for dating, 129-131
Silver ingots, **52-53,** 92-93, 102. *See also* Bullion
Silver pitchers, **136-137**
Silver Shoals, 31
Sinclair, Jim, 12, 95, 117, 143
Society of Jesus, 138
Southeast Corridor, 69, 70
Southwind, use of, in salvage operations, 49-50, 68, 70
Spain, New World empire of, 18-19, 22-24
Spangler, Joe, 71
Spinney, Hugh, 78
Stenuit, Robert, 115
Stevens, Ed, 98
Sub-bottom profiler, use of, in salvage operations, 81, 84
Summerland Key, 91-92
Sundial, recovery of, in salvage operations, **82**
Swordfish, use of, in salvage operations, 84, 90, 93, 94, 98, 99, 110, 111, 113
Swords, recovery of, in salvage operations, 55, **56-57,** 58

T

Theodolites, use of, in salvage operations, 81
Thirty Years War, 22
Tierra Firma fleet, 19, 22-23
Tilley, Lou, 49
Titanic, 115
Treasure Diver's Guide (Potter), 31, 32, 122
Treasure Salvors, 14-15, 33, 35, 36-37, 40-41, 46, 78-79, 89, 110-111, 116-117, 120-123
Trujillo, 22
Tucker, Teddy, 85
Tucker, Wendy, 104
Turks Islands, 27

U

Upper Matecumbe Key, 35
U.S.S. Monitor, 121

V

Veracruz, 19
Virgilona, use of, in salvage operations, 66, 68, 70, 77, 78, 90, 93, 94, 95, 98, 110, 113

W

Wagner, Kip, 31
Wareham, Greg, 104
Weapons
  recovery of, in salvage operations, 62, 132-133
  in 17th century, 56-57
Webber, Burt, 33, 35, 37, 46, 50-51, 54, 64, 89
Whistles, recovery of, in salvage operations, 142
Wickens, Spencer, 66, 78
Williams, Senator Dick, 31, 46, 50-51

Z

Zacharchuk, Walter, 108